Dedicated to my parents, Judith and John Woodget who taught me what is truly important in life. And who's untimely deaths in 2015 created the inciting incident that led me to create this for you.

TABLE OF CONTENTS

SECTION 1 – STORYTELLING FOR ACTION™ PLAYBOOK

SECTION 2 – 3D STORY™ FRAMEWORK STORYTELLING FOR ACTION™ PLAYBOOK

SECTION 3 - STORY MEET™ METHOD STORY MEET™ METHOD PLAYBOOK
STORYTELLING FOR ACTION™ PLAYBOOK

SECTION 4 - TRIPS STORYTELLING™ METHODOLOGY STORYTELLING FOR ACTION™ PLAYBOOK

SECTION 5 – PRESENTATION HACKS STORYTELLING FOR ACTION™ PLAYBOOK

SECTION 6 – CASE STUDIES STORY HACKS STORYTELLING FOR ACTION™ PLAYBOOK

SECTION 7 – SHORT-FORM HACKS STORYTELLING FOR ACTION™ PLAYBOOK

INTRODUCTION

GOODBYE ENTERTAINMENT STORIES
HELLO *BUSINESS* STORIES

YOUR STORY

You are living and breathing your story every day. You know that storytelling matters, that it is powerful. You know that story structures are a necessary part of how we see and communicate in the world.

You want to use storytelling in business. But doing so isn't easy. You've tried entertainment-based storytelling approaches and have become frustrated with the results they delivered.

Your day is filled with trials and tribulations that profoundly affect your life and business. And, in turn, how you interact with your customers.

These challenges are serious, and they cut to the heart of what every company seeks to do; connect to its best prospects, turn them into customers, and then into raging fans.

For customers to become raging fans, they have to choose for their story to include your story. Will you be the Obi-Wan to their Luke Skywalker?

In today's world, every product from sneakers to cloud services can be copied. Competition can catch up to our capabilities and eat our lunch at any moment.

A focus on features or benefits is no longer enough. The companies that get storytelling right create the conditions for customers to choose to include them in their story.

Our mission is to help you lead your company to craft and use your story, your company story, your product story, and your customer's stories to create a business so compelling that it's the only choice for the customers you need the most.

Storytelling for Action™ Playbooks
WHAT ARE THEY ALL ABOUT?

We designed the Storytelling for Action™ playbooks to be practical—something sorely lacking in most business storytelling advice. Storytelling for Action™ contains six main parts or 'plays.'

The first three plays deliver the basics, and practical story hacks to help you start applying them immediately. The second three playbooks help you craft real-world business deliverables using the power of storytelling.

PLAY 1

The 3D Story™ structure, you will discover the most straightforward story framework on the planet and get practice applying it to your business.

PLAY 2

The Story MeET™ method shows you how to infuse heart and soul into your stories so that people care, listen and act.

PLAY 3

Our TRIPS Storytelling™ methodology is the tool that brings alignment and consistency to all the stories you tell while ensuring they are deeply rooted in your business.

PLAY 4,5, & 6

The final three plays help you apply storytelling in a practical, day-to-day way in some of the most common deliverables we all worry about daily: presentations, case studies, and short-form content (like ads and social).

THE BIG QUESTION IS THIS:

ARE YOU READY TO TELL STORIES THAT DRIVE YOUR BUSINESS FORWARD?

Storytelling for Action™ Playbooks
HOW TO USE THEM

You want to leverage the power of business storytelling, but you don't have time to waste learning entertainment frameworks like the hero's journey.

A question I always ask when using a guide like this is, "How does it work, and what can I expect?"

HOW IT WORKS ▶

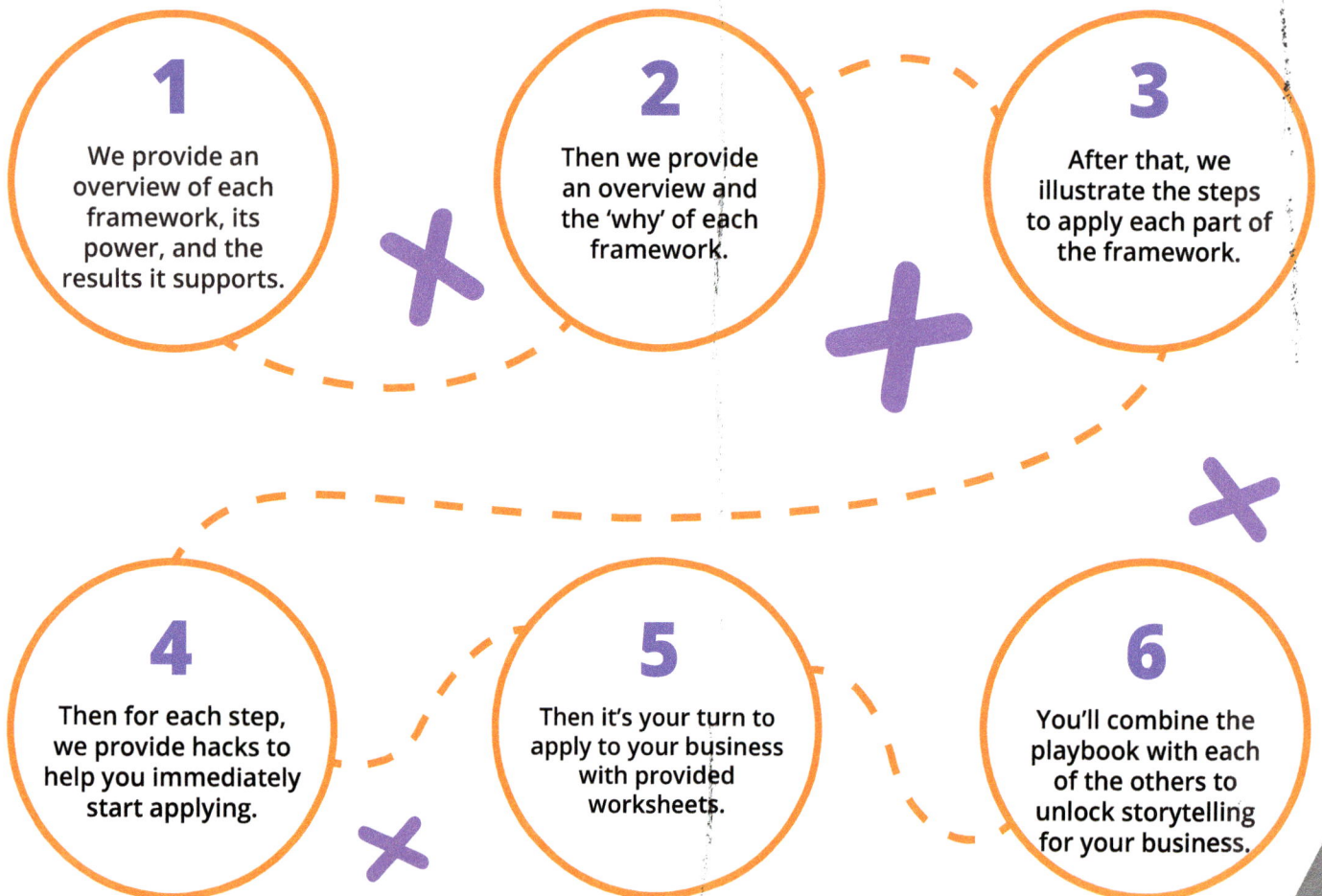

1 We provide an overview of each framework, its power, and the results it supports.

2 Then we provide an overview and the 'why' of each framework.

3 After that, we illustrate the steps to apply each part of the framework.

4 Then for each step, we provide hacks to help you immediately start applying.

5 Then it's your turn to apply to your business with provided worksheets.

6 You'll combine the playbook with each of the others to unlock storytelling for your business.

WHAT TO EXPECT

Storytelling for Action™ is a practical guide. It's not fluffy theory. Like a high-performance sports car, it's meant to be driven, not just ogled at in the garage. The playbooks provide instructions and practice to help you get the most out of your business storytelling sports car. Flow charts guide you. Hacks help you practice. Worksheets help you apply the hacks to your business. Use the playbooks to practice business storytelling, from internal meetings and office politics to campaigns and messaging.

Storytelling for Action™ Playbooks
PLAYBOOK COLLECTION

Our Storytelling For Action™ playbooks are designed as practical guides to help you benefit from the power of storytelling without becoming a storytelling expert.

Each playbook stands alone. They also work together as an all-up master playbook.

1 3D STORY™ MODEL
Tell consistent, impactful stories with this one-stop shop to telling business stories.

2 STORY MEET™ METHOD
Craft stories that engage people and retain their attention with the suitable types of emotions.

3 TRIPS STORYTELLING™ FRAMEWORK
Create aligned stories that connect to the business and drive impact.

4 STORYTELLING HACKS: PRESENTATIONS
Build presentations that move people to act even with limited time.

5 STORYTELLING HACKS: CASE STUDIES
Demonstrate social proof with customer stories without getting hung up on product details.

6 STORYTELLING HACKS: SHORT-FORM CONTENT
Make even the shortest content pop despite limited space.

OUR STORY

Like many of you, I once thought storytelling was reserved for movies, books, and theater. However, I learned that storytelling played a much more significant role in every facet of business.

My mother was a scientist — a biologist focused on virology and zoology. She encouraged my sisters and me to ask questions, develop hypotheses, and test our ideas. She taught us to seek facts. Data. Truth.

My father reinforced this, an electrical engineer who enjoyed a career spanning five decades in high-tech sales and marketing. He inadvertently indoctrinated me, resulting in first a computer science degree and later, following in his career footsteps.

Amidst this scientific and technological upbringing was a foundation of great storytelling. My parents soaked us in stories from a young age. Both my parents read to us voraciously. I still have fond memories of being curled up with dad and one of my sisters as he read us "The Lord of the Rings."

My mother, the scientist, was also a poet and author. She instilled in me a love of creative writing.

And so, I followed my mother's footsteps into creativity and my father into hi-tech when I forged a career first at Intel and then Microsoft.

SIMPLE, PRACTICAL STORYTELLING.

The mash-up of two decades in hi-tech marketing and a creative streak led to discovering simple, practical ways to apply storytelling in business. And, importantly, without all the baggage of the hero's journey or the entertainment-focused frameworks, you'll find plastered all over the internet.

We designed our Storytelling for Action™ playbooks to help you quickly start benefiting from the power of storytelling in your business. Furthermore, they are 100% focused on delivering what you need to know and nothing you don't. You won't find entertainment industry jargon in here! You will get a grounding in the foundation of the big picture and the details of storytelling, along with practical how-to's and hacks to help you start applying storytelling in business today.

I hope that after working through these playbooks, you will be rearing to go and excited to join the business storytelling revolution!

ACTION TIME!

YOUR STEPS TO SUCCESS

1 Read through each of the playbooks

2 Do a trial run – complete each playbook's worksheets

3 Use the playbooks daily to guide your business storytelling application

LET'S DO THIS!

TAKE THE PLUNGE

Start with our 3D Story™ model playbook.

Don't just use it at work. Use it this weekend with your friends and family.

Those family and friend situations are also not Hollywood and don't require the heavy hand or complexity of entertainment story frameworks. They are great situations for you to practice your business storytelling craft.

STORYTELLING FOR ACTION™

You want to create content and campaigns that are more engaging, more emotional, more valuable and more sharable.

But you're not yet confident in using storytelling as the powerful business tool that it is.

Use our Storytelling for Action™ playbooks to put storytelling to work for your business. Apply it to everything from strategy to brand to campaigns and content.

If you need further guidance, support or would like us to help you with your business storytelling please reach out to gnhelp@gonarrative.com

Copyright © Dene Strategic LLC dba Go Narrative 2021

www.GoNarrative.com

P.O. Box 16181, Seattle WA 98116

Storytelling for Action™ by Go Narrative

2022 EDITION
RECIPE AND INGREDIENTS INCLUDED.
• 14 HOW-TO FLOWS
• OVER 300 HACKS

GoNarrative
Get Attention. Be Heard. Sell More.

3D STORY™ FRAMEWORK

STORYTELLING FOR ACTION™

PLAYBOOK

TELL *CONSISTENT, IMPACTFUL STORIES* WITH THIS *ONE-STOP SHOP* TO *TELLING BUSINESS STORIES.*

WARNING:
Not for Screenwriters
or Novelists

Storytelling for Action™ Playbooks

PLAYBOOK COLLECTION

Our Storytelling For Action™ playbooks are designed as practical guides to help you benefit from the power of storytelling without becoming a storytelling expert.

Each playbook stands alone. They also work together as an all-up master playbook.

1 **3D STORY™ MODEL (THIS PLAYBOOK)**
Tell consistent, impactful stories with this one-stop shop to telling business stories.

2 **STORY MEET™ METHOD**
Craft stories that engage people and retain their attention with the suitable types of emotions.

3 **TRIPS STORYTELLING™ FRAMEWORK**
Create aligned stories that connect to the business and drive impact.

4 **STORYTELLING HACKS: PRESENTATIONS**
Build presentations that move people to act even with limited time.

5 **STORYTELLING HACKS: CASE STUDIES**
Demonstrate social proof with customer stories without getting hung up on product details.

6 **STORYTELLING HACKS: SHORT-FORM CONTENT**
Make even the shortest content pop despite limited space.

3D STORY™ FRAMEWORK

DESIRE, DIFFICULTY, DENOUEMENT

Something we hear all the time "Storytelling may be a powerful way to communicate, but I don't understand how to apply to business."

Because if anything is certain, it's that business requires communication that works.

The problem is that most advice and models were born out of hundreds of years of story-crafting in literature and the movie industries. News Flash: You're not making movies! OK, so maybe you are. And perhaps you want your customer showcase films to be as entertaining as a movie. The good news, everything you apply in this kit will help with that, too.

We didn't design these playbooks for making movies or novels. We created them for you, a businessperson, to tap into the power of storytelling, to make the most of it, and for it to have a meaningful, productive impact on your business profitability.

That's why we created the 3D Story™ framework, the world's most concise story framework. It packs a lot in while keeping it accessible and easy to remember.

DESIRE. DIFFICULTY. DENOUEMENT.

In business, people want (or need) something. This is their desire. It relates to their business, career, and personal desires. When we know what people want, we can relate to them. The thing is, nothing is ever easy in life. Am I right? There's always something in the way of getting going, getting it done, taking others on the journey. You name it, there is always a difficulty, no matter how small. When we understand the challenges, people face we can empathize with them. Empathy engenders engagement.

The way we navigate the world, the tools, processing, and approaches we use, the help we get, and the people who support us achieving our goals are the 'untangling of a knot' or denouement. This untangling is the recipe you want people to remember because when they do, they can do the same, and if it includes your product, your business wins.

These three things together are the secret code of business storytelling.

When applied, you will craft stories visible from all angles that get people to care, remember and act.

DESIRE - OVERVIEW

What does your customer want to achieve? *As the late great Steve jobs articulated,* there is a difference between wants and needs.

Wants are explicit and retained in the consciousness of your customer. They are clearly understood, and your customer has the motivation to resolve them.

Needs may not yet be explicitly known and often don't [yet] have a clearly defined want that solves for that need. For example, a customer may need to reduce a particular budget line item but may not know what they must do to create the reduction.

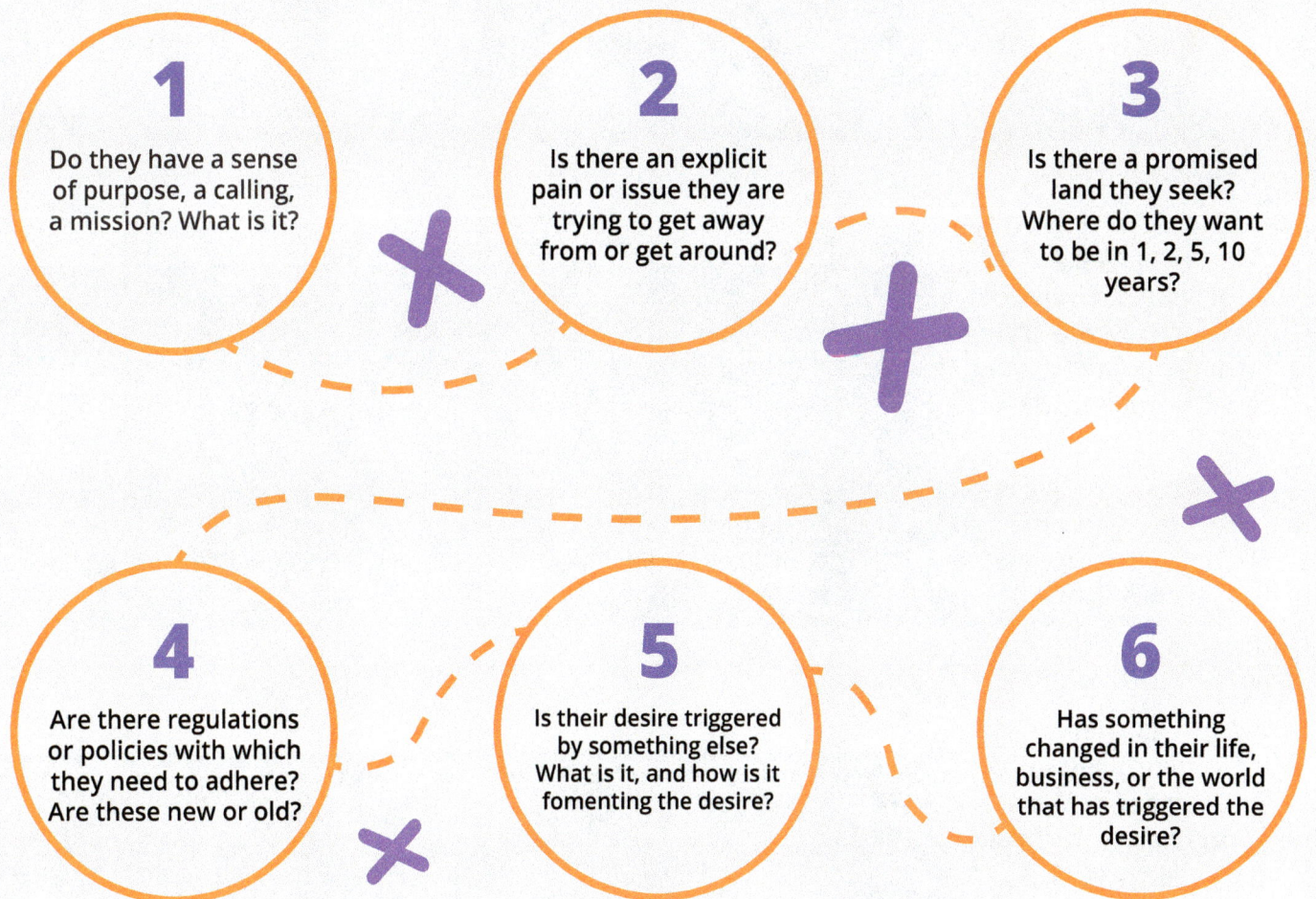

1
Do they have a sense of purpose, a calling, a mission? What is it?

2
Is there an explicit pain or issue they are trying to get away from or get around?

3
Is there a promised land they seek? Where do they want to be in 1, 2, 5, 10 years?

4
Are there regulations or policies with which they need to adhere? Are these new or old?

5
Is their desire triggered by something else? What is it, and how is it fomenting the desire?

6
Has something changed in their life, business, or the world that has triggered the desire?

Consider this 'panning for gold.' You are exploring the driving force behind your buyer's story. Story talks to story. So you need to understand theirs. What do they want? What will make them happy?

Storytelling for Action™ Playbooks
DESIRE - HACKS

Do they have a sense of purpose, a calling, a mission? What is it?

- Helping others succeed.
- Improving the environment or world.
- Improving quality of life, business (themselves, others).
- To be trustworthy and authentic.
- To inspire others.
- To provide for others.

Is there an explicit pain or issue they are trying to get away from or get around?

- People are not listening to our message.
- There are forces and money fighting us.
- The people we try to help don't understand why they should change.
- Brand has historic negative baggage.
- Lack of trust.
- Scarcity or cost of resources.

Is there a promised land they seek? Where do they want to be in 1, 2, 5, 10 years?

- Positive sentiment, unsolicited feedback.
- Reduction of a negative number.
- Customer satisfaction scores, NSAT, NPS.
- Ratings on public websites (e.g., G2 Crowd).
- Social sharing, views, clicks.
- Financial success.

HACKS

Are there regulations or policies with which they need to adhere? Are these new or old?

- Government regulations.
    - (e.g., Environmental standards)
- Data and privacy requirements.
- ISO Standards.
- Best practices or methods established by other entities.

Is their desire triggered by something else? What is it, and how is it fomenting the desire?

- Receiving or being nominated for an award.
- Employee demands.
- Shifts in public sentiment or perception.
    - (#CampaignHashtag)
- Acquisitions of products or business that are relied on.
- Bankruptcies.
- Industry, individual, or ecosystem risks (e.g., Asbestos).

Has something changed in their life, business, or the world that has triggered the desire?

- Social media and self-image.
- The space race inspired a generation of scientists.
- The Dot Com era inspired new business models.

Storytelling for Action™ Playbooks
DESIRE – WORKSHEET

Do they have a sense of purpose, a calling, a mission? What is it?

Is there an explicit pain or issue they are trying to get away from or get around?

Is there a promised land they seek? Where do they want to be in 1, 2, 5, 10 years?

WORK

Are there regulations or policies with which they need to adhere? Are these new or old?

Is their desire triggered by something else? What is it, and how is it fomenting the desire?

Has something changed in their life, business, or the world that has triggered the desire?

DIFFICULTY - OVERVIEW

If only we could always get what we wanted in life. If we could, there would be no stories, and the world would be a boring place.

Difficulty is about what stands in the way of your customer achieving their desire. It could be specific, or it could be situational.

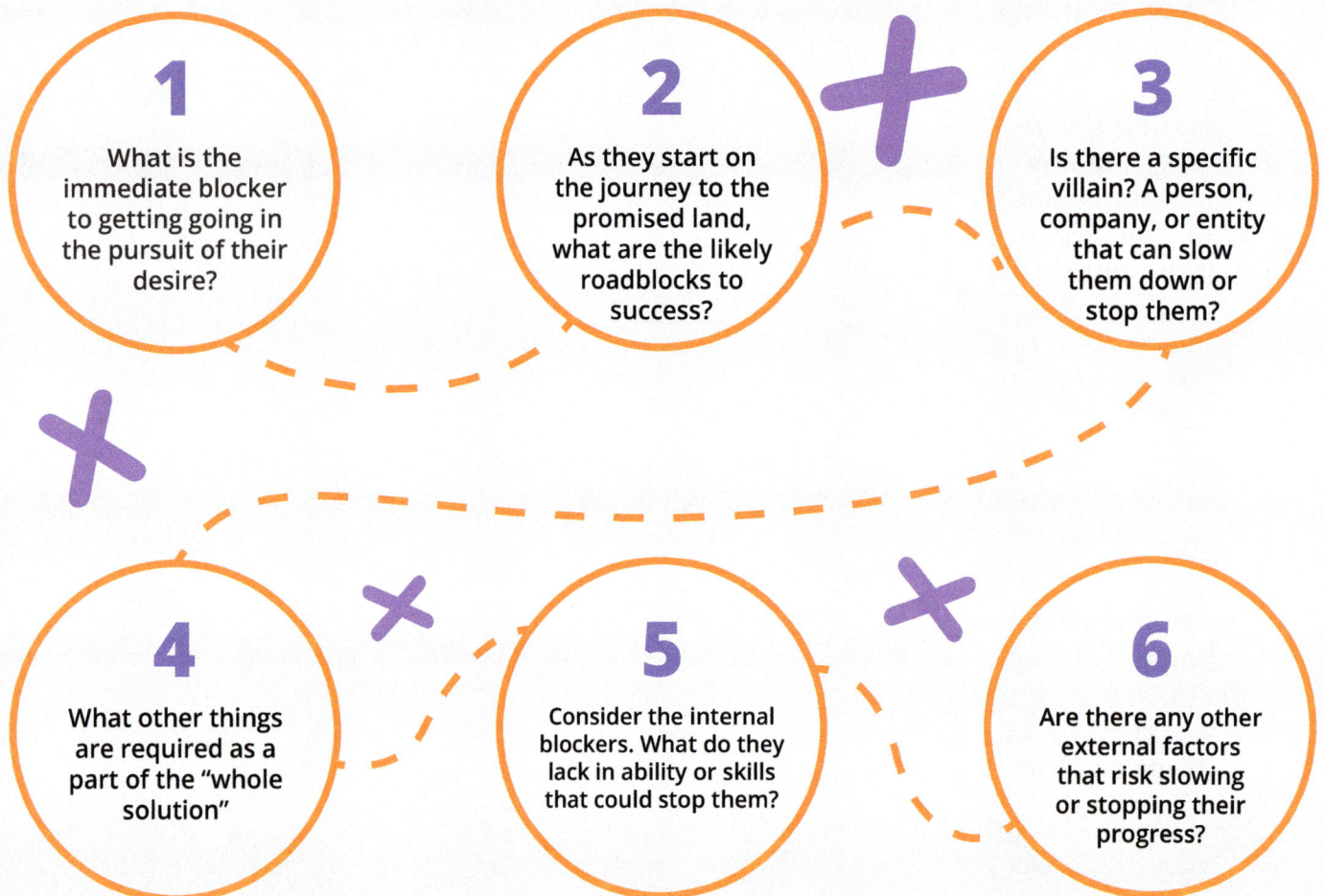

1 What is the immediate blocker to getting going in the pursuit of their desire?

2 As they start on the journey to the promised land, what are the likely roadblocks to success?

3 Is there a specific villain? A person, company, or entity that can slow them down or stop them?

4 What other things are required as a part of the "whole solution"

5 Consider the internal blockers. What do they lack in ability or skills that could stop them?

6 Are there any other external factors that risk slowing or stopping their progress?

Particular issues are immediate and direct. Situational problems are about the whole product and the other environmental aspects that all accrue to a roadblock between your customer and their success.

Furthermore, a difficultly could be internal (lack of skills) or external (competitor behavior).

Be mindful of getting too 'into the weeds.' Focus on the most significant issues, prioritize, and select.

Even something as simple as getting a glass of water contains things that must be overcome. A mundane example could be; you're on a call in your home office and suddenly get thirsty. The other end of the spectrum is when someone in drought conditions must walk miles to get water. Spend some time wallowing in what the challenges could be.

Storytelling for Action™ Playbooks
DIFFICULTY – HACKS

What is the immediate blocker to getting going in the pursuit of their desire?

- Perceived high cost.
- Lots of options causing analysis paralysis.
- Lack of social proof.
- Too busy.
- Approvals processes.
- Company Culture.

As they start on the journey to the promised land, what are the likely roadblocks to success?

- Integration challenges (getting a solution to work with other things).
- Complexity.
- Large amount of time required to deploy, integrate or get running.
- Permissions or access levels.

Is there a specific villain? A person, company, or entity that can slow them down or stop them?

- Manager or other financial signatory authority.
- Internal politics.
- Another team, it's manager or a vocal detractor.
- Disgruntled colleague .
- Competitors (especially those who are fast-moving).
- Politicians or political movements or protestors.

What other things are required as a part of the "whole solution"

- Specific device or system ("the app is only available on iPhone").
- Required third party services.
- Up-to-date systems or infrastructure .

Consider the internal blockers. What do they lack in ability or skills that could stop them?

- Lack of confidence.
- Lack of skills or experience.
- Credentials or licenses.
- Trust.
- Fear.
- Uncertainty or doubt about their abilities.

Are there any other external factors that risk slowing or stopping their progress?

- Weather or other Seasonality.
- Demographics.
- Cyber risks or attacks.
- The economy.
- Geographic factors.
- Government and regulations.

Storytelling for Action™ Playbooks
DIFFICULTY - WORKS

What is the immediate blocker to getting going in the pursuit of their desire?

As they start on the journey to the promised land, what are the likely roadblocks to success?

Is there a specific villain? A person, company, or entity that can slow them down or stop them?

What other things are required as a part of the "whole solution"

Consider the internal blockers. What do they lack in ability or skills that could stop them?

Are there any other external factors that risk slowing or stopping their progress?

DENOUEMENT.
.OVERVIEW

———

A French word meaning the "untangling of the knot." What key benefits of your product helps to solve the difficulty and enable your customer to achieve their desired end state?

Your objective here is to capture how things can and will be better for your customer with your product or service in the picture.

For example, something you do or offer that results in simplification, confidence building, cost reduction, or help to get the job done.

There are likely dozens of features, benefits, and capabilities of your product, service, or program. What are the top one, two, or three that help with the most significant roadblocks?

1
How did they approach overcoming the roadblocks or navigate the experience?

2
What were the results that they were able to celebrate?

3
How did they change or transform personally, their business?

4
What third-party components were required as a part of a "complete solution."

5
What was learned or "taken away" from the experience?

6
What, specifically, is it what your product or service did to help?

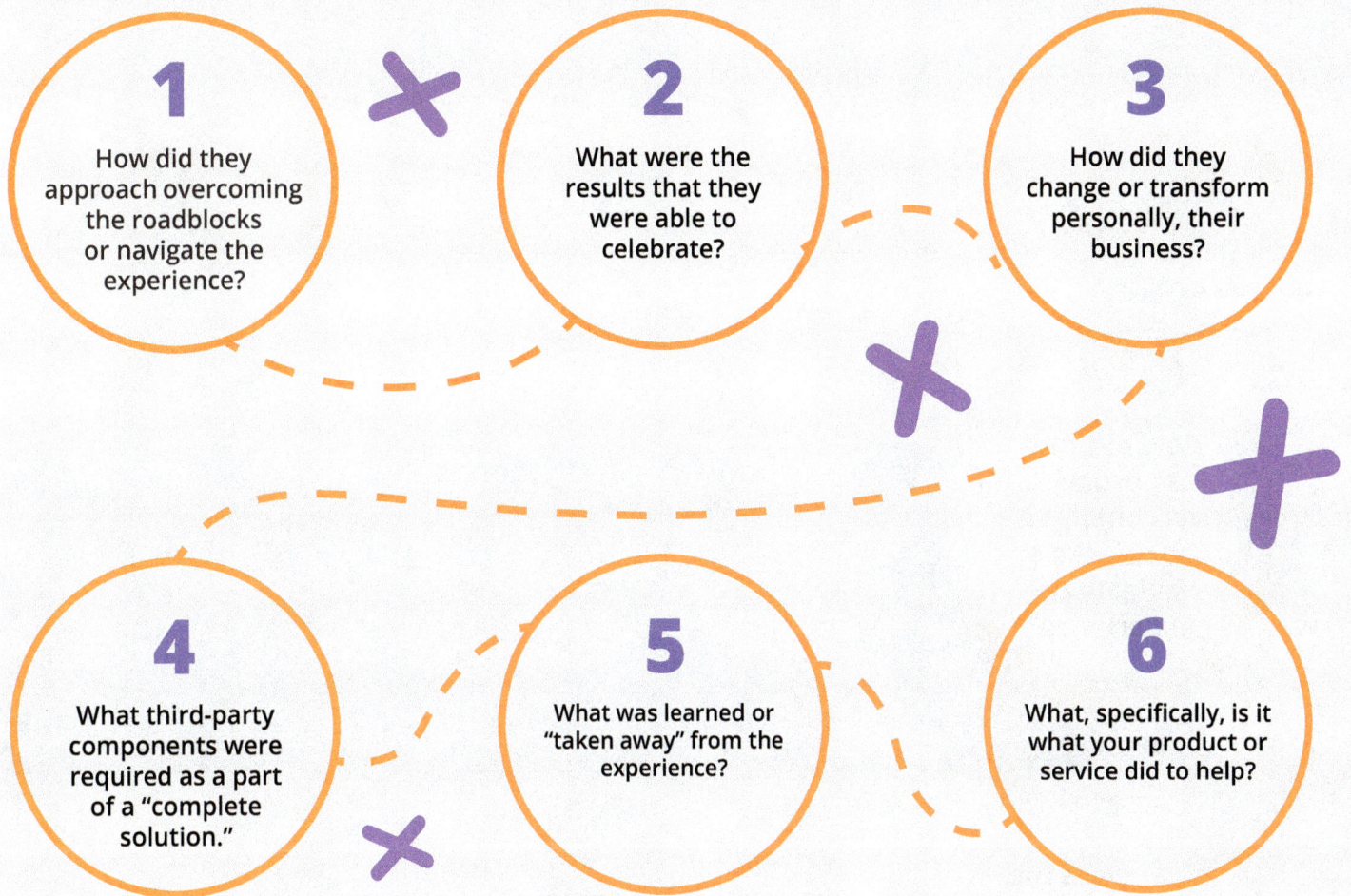

We like to keep our language simple. So why the complicated, hard to pronounce French word? We fell in love with it's meaning "the untangling of a knot" because it is a metaphor, and we love metaphors! Especially ones that do such a great job as a short cut to understanding.

DENOUEMENT

Storytelling for Action™ Playbooks
DENOUEMENT – HACKS

How did they approach overcoming the roadblocks or navigate the experience?

- The steps and sequence they took.
- Recipes or guides that were followed.
- Other people, roles that were involved.
- What was fast or slow about the experience?

What were the results that they were able to celebrate?

- Growth in users, revenue, subscriptions.
- Viral coefficient, likes, shares.
- Net Promoter Score (NPS).
- Compound Annual Growth Rate (CAGR).
- Specific customer feedback.
- Increase or decrease in a metric.

How did they change or transform personally, their business?

- They are now better at...
- Increase in confidence.
- Freed from prior constraints.
- They no longer have to deal with....
- Something or someone is faster or slower.
- New opportunities were opened up.

MENT

What third-party components are required as a part of a "complete solution."

- Software, cloud services.
- Hardware, devices, or machinery.
- Consumables or commodities.
- Services.
- Training programs.
- Books, literature.

What was learned or "taken away" from the experience?

- Increase in awareness.
- Education goals, continuing education credits.
- Best practices or "must-dos" to follow when doing it.
- Things to avoid when doing it.

What, specifically, is it what your product or service does to help?

- How it helped with one of the specific difficulties.
- How it was used and why.
- Select only features relevant to helping solve the specific difficulty with this particular story, even if your product can do much more.

Storytelling for Action™ Playbooks

DENOUEMENT – WORK

How did they approach overcoming the roadblocks or navigate the experience?

What were the results that they were able to celebrate?

How did they change or transform personally, their business?

HEET MENT

What third-party components are required as a part of a "complete solution."

What was learned or "taken away" from the experience?

What, specifically, is it what your product or service does to help?

GoNarrative
Get Attention. Be Heard. Sell More.

2022 EDITION
RECIPE AND
INGREDIENTS INCLUDED
• 14 HOW-TO FLOW
• OVER 300 HACK

STORY MEET™ METHOD
STORYTELLING FOR ACTION™
PLAYBOOK

CRAFT STORIES THAT *ENGAGE PEOPLE* AND *RETAIN THEIR ATTENTION* WITH THE RIGHT TYPES OF EMOTIONS.

WARNING:
Not for Screenwriters
or Novelists

Storytelling for Action™ Playbooks

PLAYBOOK COLLECTION

Our Storytelling For Action™ playbooks are designed as practical guides to help you benefit from the power of storytelling without becoming a storytelling expert.

Each playbook stands alone. They also work together as an all-up master playbook.

1 ### 3D STORY™ MODEL
Tell consistent, impactful stories with this one-stop shop to telling business stories.

2 ### STORY MEET™ METHOD (THIS PLAYBOOK)
Craft stories that engage people and retain their attention with the suitable types of emotions.

3 ### TRIPS STORYTELLING™ FRAMEWORK
Create aligned stories that connect to the business and drive impact.

4 ### STORYTELLING HACKS: PRESENTATIONS
Build presentations that move people to act even with limited time.

5 ### STORYTELLING HACKS: CASE STUDIES
Demonstrate social proof with customer stories without getting hung up on product details.

6 ### STORYTELLING HACKS: SHORT-FORM CONTENT
Make even the shortest content pop despite limited space.

STORY MEET™ METHOD - OVERVIEW
MORALS, ESSENTIAL EMOTIONS, TRUTHS

A story requires heart, emotion. Go beyond products and even storylines to explore what makes your audience tick. What is important to them? How do they see the world? What framing will help you engage with them in a meaningful way?

Morals are the guardrails by which people live. They govern our behavior. What will or won't your customer do to maintain their integrity?

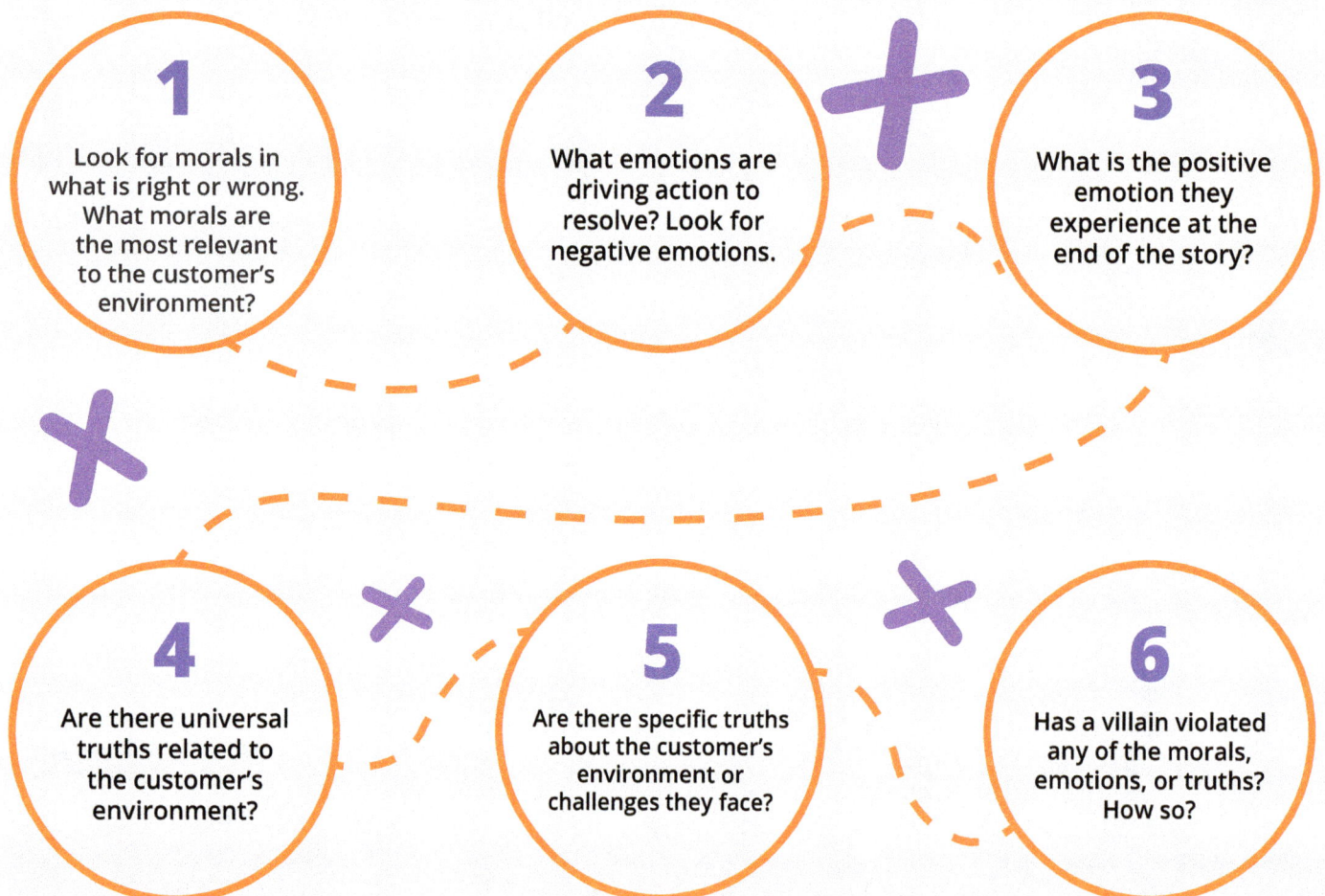

1 Look for morals in what is right or wrong. What morals are the most relevant to the customer's environment?

2 What emotions are driving action to resolve? Look for negative emotions.

3 What is the positive emotion they experience at the end of the story?

4 Are there universal truths related to the customer's environment?

5 Are there specific truths about the customer's environment or challenges they face?

6 Has a villain violated any of the morals, emotions, or truths? How so?

ESSENTIAL EMOTIONS

Essential Emotions relate to the feelings people have about the situation they are in and the place they end up. Emotions fuel our decision-making process.

People see the world through a lens (sometimes rose-colored) informed by the Truths they hold. There are also universal truths: truths shape perception, reaction, response, and action.

We believe in meeting customers where they are. This requires understanding and empathy. Time to get out of the box of features and benefits and see the world through your customers' eyes.

Storytelling for Action™ Playbooks
STORY MEET™ – HACKS

Look for morals in what is right or wrong. What morals are the most relevant to the customer's environment?

- Tell the truth.
- Be tolerant and inclusive.
- Be humble.
- Treat others as you wish to be treated
- Keep promises.
- Be patient.
- Have integrity.

What emotions are driving action to resolve? Look for negative emotions.

- Fear and Anxiety.
- Hope.
- Frustration.
- Denial.
- Worry.
- Fascination.
- Vulnerability.

What is the positive emotion they experience at the end of the story?

- Confident.
- Enthusiastic.
- Grateful.
- Happy.
- Appreciative.

EET ™ —

Are there universal truths related to the customer's environment?

- Stress.
- Happiness is fleeting.
- Our choice dictate our outcomes.
- Trust your gut.
- Born equal, leave equal.
- Helping others leads to fulfillment.

Are there specific truths about the customer's environment or challenges they face?

- Failure results in learning.
- You won't know if you don't try.
- How we were raised.
- We want to be accepted.
- "We've always done it this way."
- "We don't do that here."

Has a villain violated any of the morals, emotions, or truths? How so?

- Manager, leader.
- Competitor.
- Hacker. Spearphisher.
- Thief.
- Prior vendor.
- Partner gone wrong.

Storytelling for Action™ Playbooks
STORY MEET™ – WORK

Look for morals in what is right or wrong. What morals are the most relevant to the customer's environment?

What emotions are driving action to resolve? Look for negative emotions.

What is the positive emotion they experience at the end of the story?

EET™

HEET

Are there universal truths related to the customer's environment?

Are there specific truths about the customer's environment or challenges they face?

Has a villain violated any of the morals, emotions, or truths? How so?

GoNarrative
Get Attention. Be Heard. Get More.

TRIPS STORYTELLING™ METHODOLOGY
STORYTELLING FOR ACTION™ PLAYBOOK

CREATE **ALIGNED STORIES** THAT **CONNECT** TO THE **BUSINESS** AND **DRIVE IMPACT.**

WARNING:
Not for Screenwriters
or Novelists

Storytelling for Action™ Playbooks

PLAYBOOK COLLECTION

Our Storytelling For Action™ playbooks are designed as practical guides to help you benefit from the power of storytelling without becoming a storytelling expert.

Each playbook stands alone. They also work together as an all-up master playbook.

1 ### 3D STORY™ MODEL
Tell consistent, impactful stories with this one-stop shop to telling business stories.

2 ### STORY MEET™ METHOD
Craft stories that engage people and retain their attention with the suitable types of emotions.

3 ### TRIPS STORYTELLING™ FRAMEWORK (THIS PLAYBOOK)
Create aligned stories that connect to the business and drive impact.

4 ### STORYTELLING HACKS: PRESENTATIONS
Build presentations that move people to act even with limited time.

5 ### STORYTELLING HACKS: CASE STUDIES
Demonstrate social proof with customer stories without getting hung up on product details.

6 ### STORYTELLING HACKS: SHORT-FORM CONTENT
Make even the shortest content pop despite limited space.

TRIPS STORYTELLING™ METHODOLOGY OVERVIEW

TRANSFORMATION, REASONS, INNOVATION, PROBLEMS, STORIES

A story is about something that happens to someone. In nature, when there is a pattern with multiple stories that share a common message, we call this a narrative and give it a metaphor.

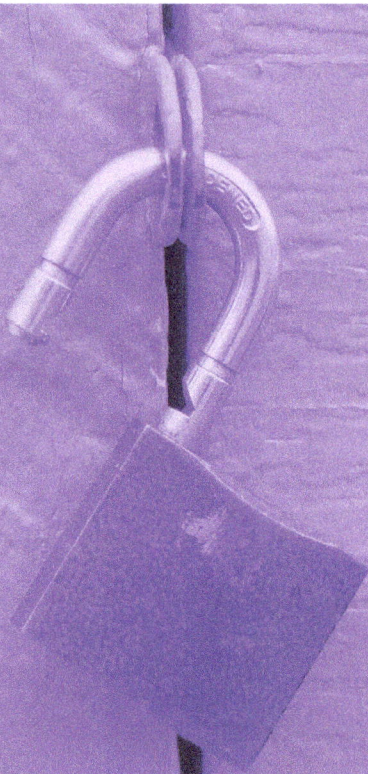

"The self-made person" is born out of the stories of entrepreneurs and explorers. "They who dare, win" comes from people taking risks and finding great success.

We use narrative to frame a story, give it direction, and bring consistency to a collection of stories.

When armed with this knowledge, you can reverse engineer a narrative. A practice many will be familiar with from politics or international relations.

By identifying the specific traits of the topic at hand, you can select a narrative message grounded in specifics.

Your tailored and strategic narrative will enable you to share all the stories you tell with consistency and clarity with a firm foundation.

Furthermore, it informs your mission, vision, and even product development when you are clear on your narrative. A strategic narrative is the best way to build integrity and alignment within and outside your organization.

TRANSFORMATION - OVERVIEW

"Most of us are about as eager to be changed as we were to be born and go through our changes in a similar state of shock" - James A Baldwin.

The world is continuously changing; this fact is inescapable. As it shifts, it puts forces on us to which we must adapt. We seek tips, tricks, and tools to navigate these changes.

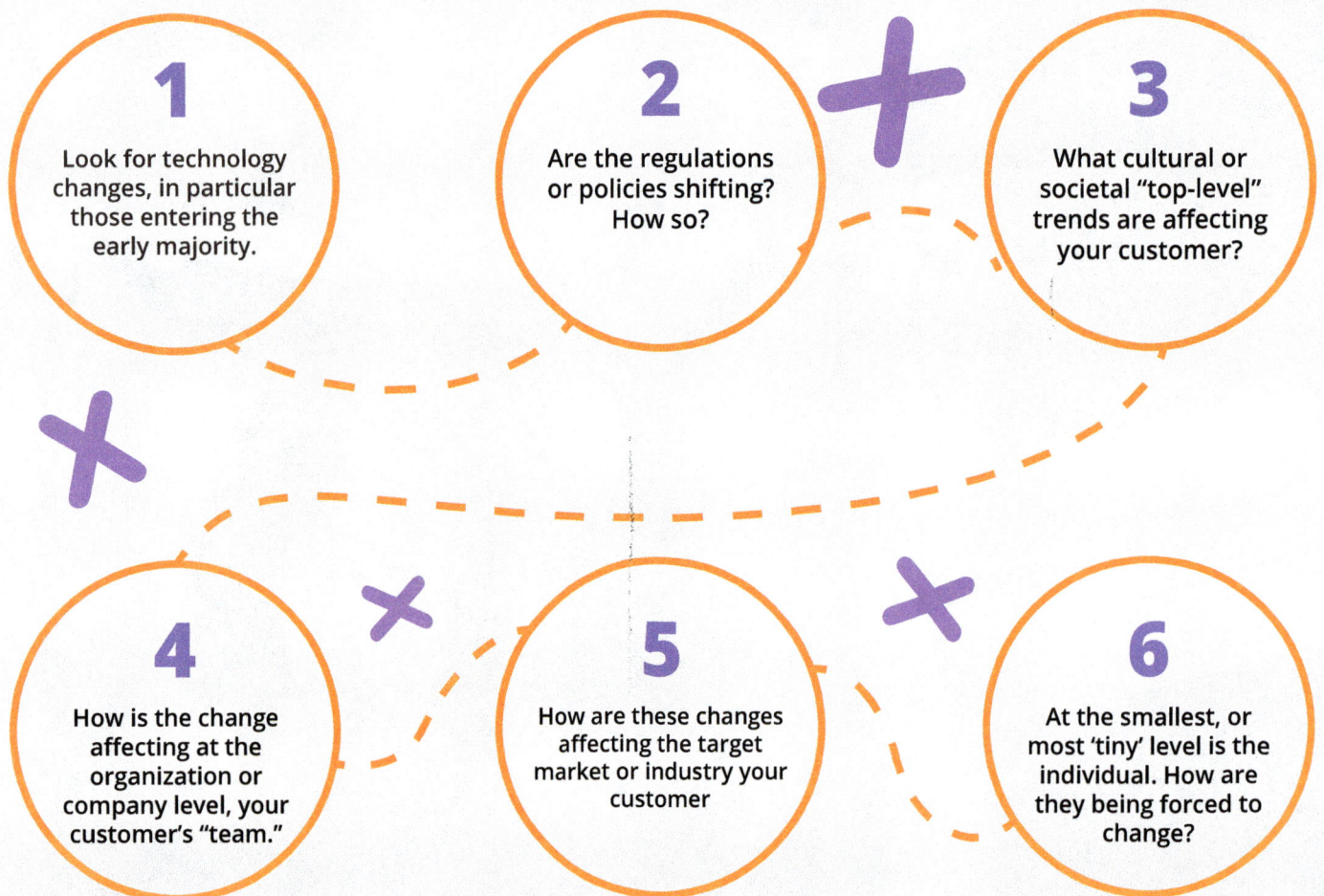

1
Look for technology changes, in particular those entering the early majority.

2
Are the regulations or policies shifting? How so?

3
What cultural or societal "top-level" trends are affecting your customer?

4
How is the change affecting at the organization or company level, your customer's "team."

5
How are these changes affecting the target market or industry your customer

6
At the smallest, or most 'tiny' level is the individual. How are they being forced to change?

Like inertia and Newton's First Law, people do not change unless an outside force acts upon them. What transformation(s) are going on in the market? In your customers' lives? What changes are occurring? What pressure is being put on your customers' to adapt?

These can happen at a top-level, target market level, team level, or 'tiny' (atomic, individual) level.

Consider the associated risks and opportunities with the change. Will hanging on to the status quo leave your customers behind? Eventually, the status quo becomes history.

Are the imposed changes forcing a reactive effect or inspiring proactive opportunity seizing?

Storytelling for Action™ Playbooks
TRANSFORMATION – H

Look for technology changes, in particular those entering the early majority.

- Increase in speed or efficiency.
- Consolidation of features (e.g., cameras in phones).
- Shift from ownership to service or lease (e.g., cloud computing).
- Disruption (e.g., digital camera vs. film).
- Supplemental approaches (e.g., digital payments vs. credit cards).

Are the regulations or policies shifting? How so?

- Environmental (e.g., clean water laws, Paris accord).
- Intellectual and corporate law (e.g., copyright law, antitrust law).
- Healthcare (e.g., Affordable Care Act).
- Privacy laws (e.g., GDPR, CCPA).
- Government subsidies (e.g., clean energy, farming).

What cultural or societal "top-level" trends are affecting your customer?

- Changes in urbanization, gentrification, migration.
- Health and safety (e.g., COVID19).
- Social justice (e.g., affirmative action, free public education).
- Shifting fashions (what's in or out?).

How is the change affecting at the organization or company level, your customer's "team."

- Supply and demand is increasing/decreasing.
- Supply chain disruption (e.g., regional conflict).
- A sector has growth unleashed/restricted.
- Increasing cost pressure on commodities and cost of goods sold.
- Customer preferences force change (e.g., shift to SUVs from sedans).

How are these changes affecting the target market or industry your customer

- Profitability is impacted (positive, negative).
- Companies put out of business (local retail vs. Amazon).
- Change in service delivery (dine-in vs. delivery).
- New markets or channels opened (e.g., social media advertising).

At the smallest, or most 'tiny' level is the individual. How are they being forced to change?

- Risk to job security.
- Imposed reskilling.
- Empowerment.
- New career opportunities.
- Increased ability to focus on meaningful work.
- How consumers purchase (e.g., online vs. brick and mortar).

Storytelling for Action™ Playbooks
TRANSFORMATION – W

Look for technology changes, in particular those entering the early majority.

Are the regulations or policies shifting? How so?

What cultural or societal "top-level" trends are affecting your customer?

RKSHEET

How is the change affecting at the organization or company level, your customer's "team."

How are these changes affecting the target market or industry your customer

At the smallest, or most 'tiny' level is the individual. How are they being forced to change?

REASONS (TO BELIEVE - OVERVIEW

"People with high levels of personal mastery... cannot afford to choose between reason and intuition, or head and heart, any more than they would choose to walk on one leg or see with one eye." – Peter Senge

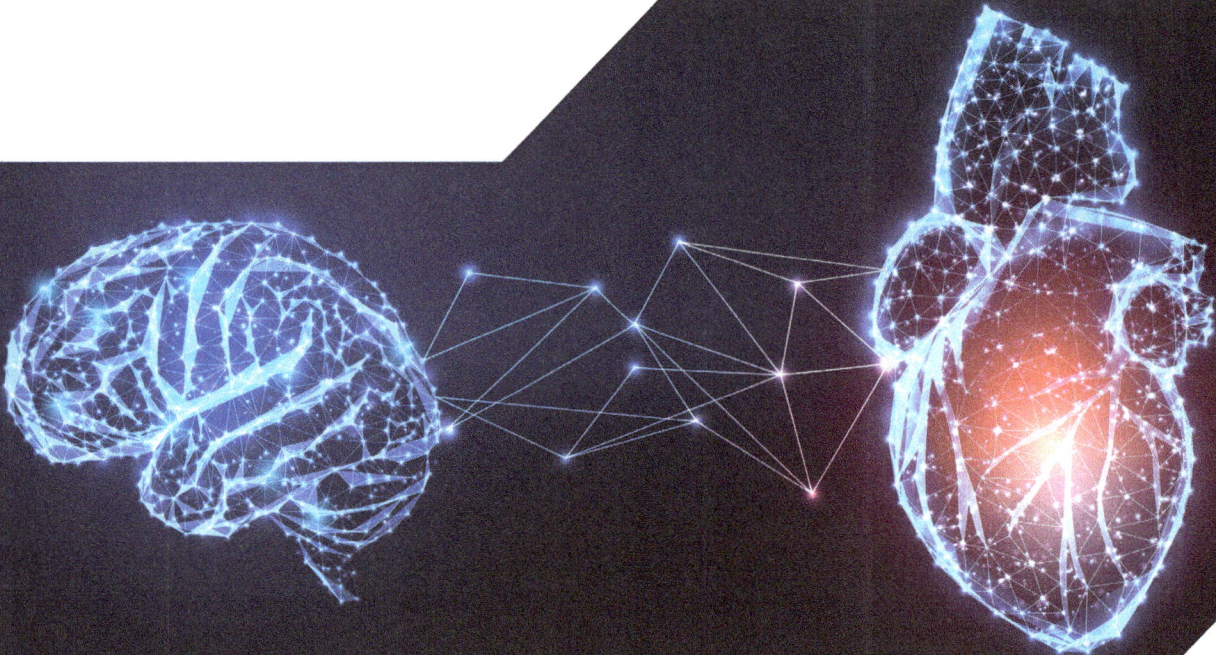

Think of the reasons for the head and the heart.

For the head, consider what supports believing you? What can you cite as motivators driving the change? Facts. Trends. Data.

For the heart, consider the why, the motivation, and audience aspirations or inspiration. What excellent end-state awaits at the end of the rainbow for those that successfully navigate the transformation?

BELIEVE) -

1
What are the trends, the facts, the figures that serve as proof points for the transformation?

2
What's the urgency? What are the time frames involved?

3
What are the experts saying about it?

4
How is it being covered in the press?

5
Achievement opportunities that the transformation creates

6
What is the opportunity cost of not embarking on the change?

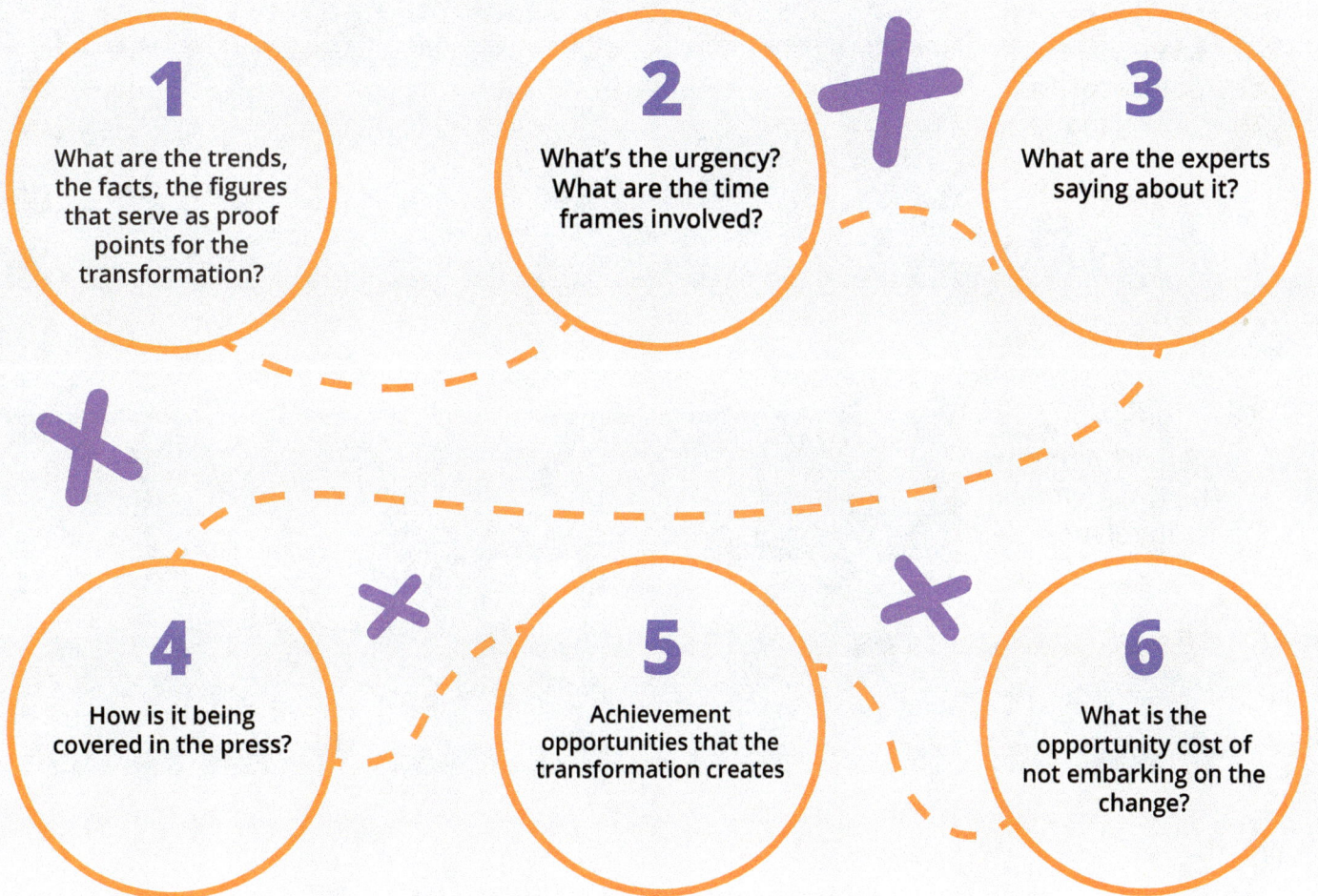

Is there an opportunity cost? What will they lose if they do not embark?

Transformation is all very well and good, but remember, people, don't like change. They won't change unless they must. A justification could be a fact or figure that triggers the need to act when added to their story. Or it could be an emotional or inspirational reason that mainlines the need for change. What will they miss out on if they don't tackle the change?

Storytelling for Action™ Playbooks
REASONS TO BELIEVE

What are the trends, the facts, the figures that serve as proof points for the transformation?

- Increase or decrease in the availability of a resource.
- Measurable impact articulated in amount or percentage changes.
- Shifts in production, consumption or trade e.g., increasing shift from gasoline to electric cars.
- Increase or decrease in timeframes e.g., rendering of movie special effects, ore mining extraction rates.

What's the urgency? What are the time frames involved?

- How fast or slow are these changes taking place? Accelerating?
- Is the change a known shift that is slow or lagging?
- Is the change new and an opportunity for first-mover advantage?
- Is the change something that has recently accelerated?
- How soon will associated risks play out? Act now? Wait for a bit?

What are the experts saying about it?

- Is there a research paper that articulates the change?
- What scientific or technological innovations are fueling the change?
- What are universities or Ph.D.'s saying about the change?
- How are analysts framing it with existing technology and markets?

HACKS TO BE

How is it being covered in the press?

- What press coverage is there?
- What are popular bloggers or podcasters saying about the change?
- Are there any big brands making moves to capitalize? Smaller ones?
- Is the change framed as inherently good or bad? About capitalizing on an opportunity or about avoiding a risk?
- What is the social dialog saying (Reddit, Twitter)?

Achievement opportunities that the transformation creates.

- What are potential inspirational or aspirational end-states?
- What new opportunities exist for those who embrace the change?
- How did early adopters fair? Adapt? Capitalize? Minimize risk?
- What is increased by embracing? Decreased by not? Sales? Growth?
- What emotions are expressed by those who are embracing it?
- Are there associated additional, possibly hidden positive benefits?

What is the opportunity cost of not embarking on the change?

- What risks are associated with avoiding or delaying adapting?
- How will people/organizations who avoid the change be left behind?
- Increase in difficulty by lagging? (e.g., leaded fuel car needs additive)
- What becomes impossible? e.g., dial up internet PC = no internet?
- Will their status be reduced?

Storytelling for Action™ Playbooks
REASONS TO BELIEVE

What are the trends, the facts, the figures that serve as proof points for the transformation?

What's the urgency? What are the time frames involved?

What are the experts saying about it?

WORKSHEET

How is it being covered in the press?

Achievement opportunities that the transformation creates.

What is the opportunity cost of not embarking on the change?

INNOVATION - OVERVIEW

────

"This is the weapon of a Jedi Knight. Not as clumsy or random as a blaster; an elegant weapon for a more civilized age." – Obi-Wan Kenobi

What's unique about your offering? Not the "table-stakes." Special. This isn't about sharing all that you can do or all your product's features or service capabilities.

What is it, specifically, that you deliver that helps us navigate this transformation? Why should we choose you?

How do you help people, teams, and companies survive the transformation? Or help them

1 What is your killer feature or capability?

2 What is it about your "whole product" that makes you the best choice?

3 What is it about your company or people that makes you a great choice?

4 What else is special about you that makes you irresistible?

5 How do you help them achieve a better end state? What outstanding positive outcomes you directly enable?

6 Who or what is your competition and why should we choose you instead?

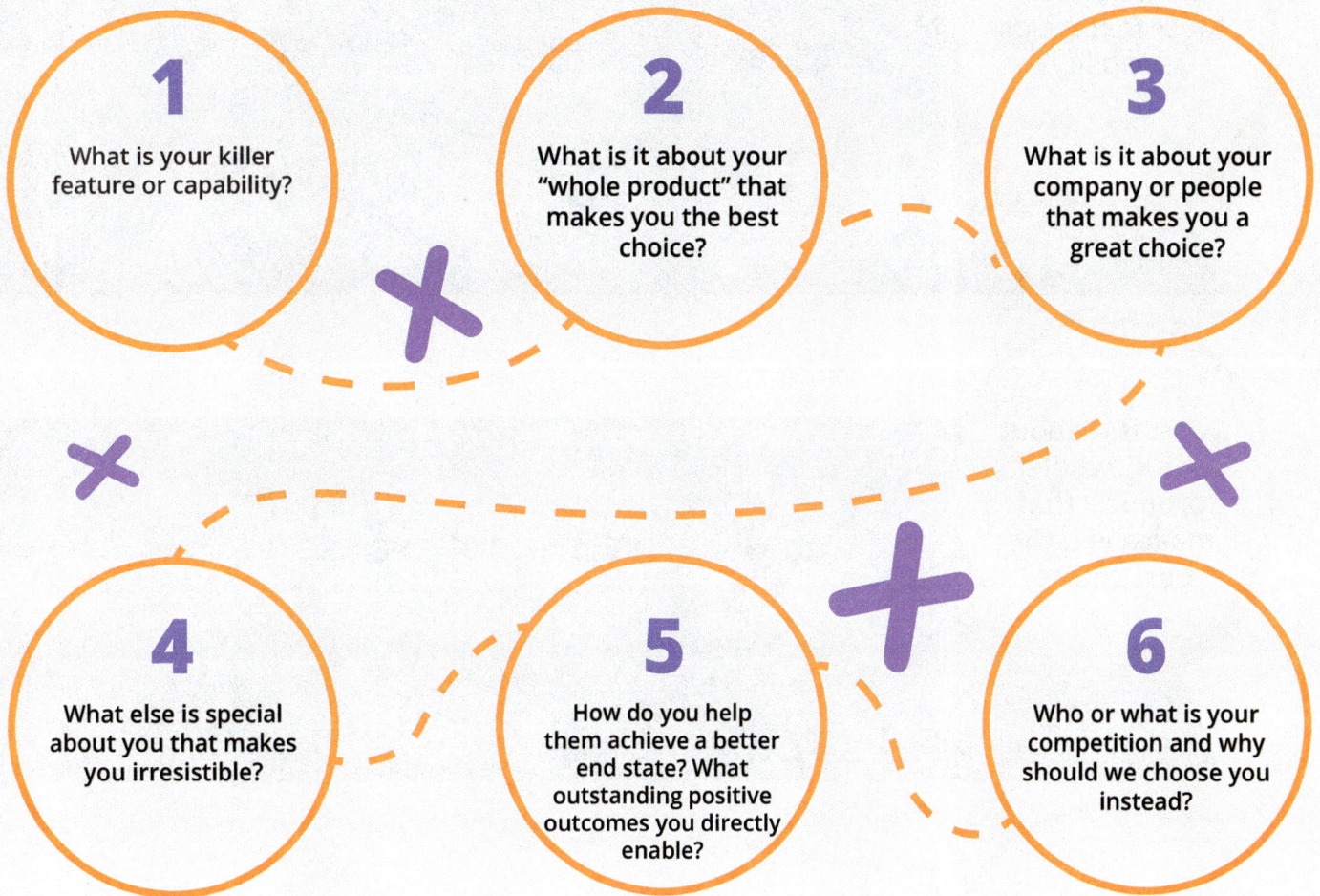

capitalize on it? Or help them become more connected or efficient because of it?

The risk with talking about ourselves is we can always do much, much more than just one thing. And because of this, we fall into the trap of sharing too much. This exercise is about hunting for that one, two, maybe three at the most things that together only you bring to the world. Frame everything as it relates to the best possible customer experience.

Storytelling for Action™ Playbooks
INNOVATION - HACKS

What is your killer feature or capability?

- A feature or benefit that only you provide.
- The patents that fuel your products.
- The highest priority feature in your sea of capability.
- This isn't about every capability. What makes your offering special?

What is it about your "whole product" that makes you the best choice?

- Ecosystem integration (APIs, Partnerships, Zapier).
- Integration with other products/services you offer.
- How it's sold/where it's available (more available?).
- Onboarding, resources, training & customer experiences.
- Do you have a particularly easy implementation or deployment?
- Do you offer free trials? Without providing credit card information?

What is it about your company or people that makes you a great choice?

- Customer experience, customer success track record?
- Do you offer free delivery (and return) or installation?
- Do you have an outstanding return policy (e.g., lifetime).
- Company values and alignment with specific audience values.

TION —

What else is special about you that makes you irresistible?

- Is what you offer delivered in a unique or special way?
- Did your founder climb a mountain to bring customers this treasure?
- Any past success or proof of achievement in a relevant space.
- Do you have more heart? Perhaps your product or service helped an underserved or disenfranchised community.

How do you help them achieve a better end state? What outstanding positive outcomes you directly enable?

- Do you get them there quicker? How much faster are you?
- Safety and confidence. Which risk do you mitigate best?
- Help people compete. Which opportunity do you accelerate?
- Secret weapon. Do you help clients compete more effectively?

Who or what is your competition and why should we choose you instead?

- Do you offer a more complete experience?
- Cost savings. Do you eliminate the need for and make redundant other [expensive] products or services?
- Versatility. Do you enable the opportunity to use complementary third-party services that are best-in-class
- Better. Faster. Stronger. What's the multiplier? 10X, 100X?
- Are people happier when they do it with your company?

Storytelling for Action™ Playbooks
INNOVATION - WORKS

What is your killer feature or capability?

What is it about your "whole product" that makes you the best choice?

What is it about your company or people that makes you a great choice?

What else is special about you that makes you irresistible?

How do you help them achieve a better end state? What outstanding positive outcomes you directly enable?

Who or what is your competition and why should we choose you instead?

PROBLEMS - OVERVIEW

"After months of want and hunger, we suddenly found ourselves able to have meals fit for the gods, and with appetites, the gods might have envied." – Ernest Shackleton.

Problems are interesting.

Problems are at the heart of good storytelling. They create a contrast. Before, after. Slower, faster. Fear, safety.

Problems relate deeply to transformation and change. An issue not addressed or overcome is a transformation never realized—a tragedy. Solving even the slightest problems (being hungry, for example) results in a change if resolved (feeling full and content).

Did we think life was going to be easy? No! Can we wave our magic wand and make everybody happy. Not so fast! Problems always arise. What stands in your customer's way as they try and navigate the transformation?

1

What problems does the transformation create or impose?

2

What issues are there getting going or starting to tackle the transformation?

3

What common roadblocks exist for people tackling the change?

4

What additional problems are triggered on the journey?

5

What is lost by not embarking on the transformation? Opportunity cost.

6

What are the internal problems, or struggles with embarking on and navigating the change?

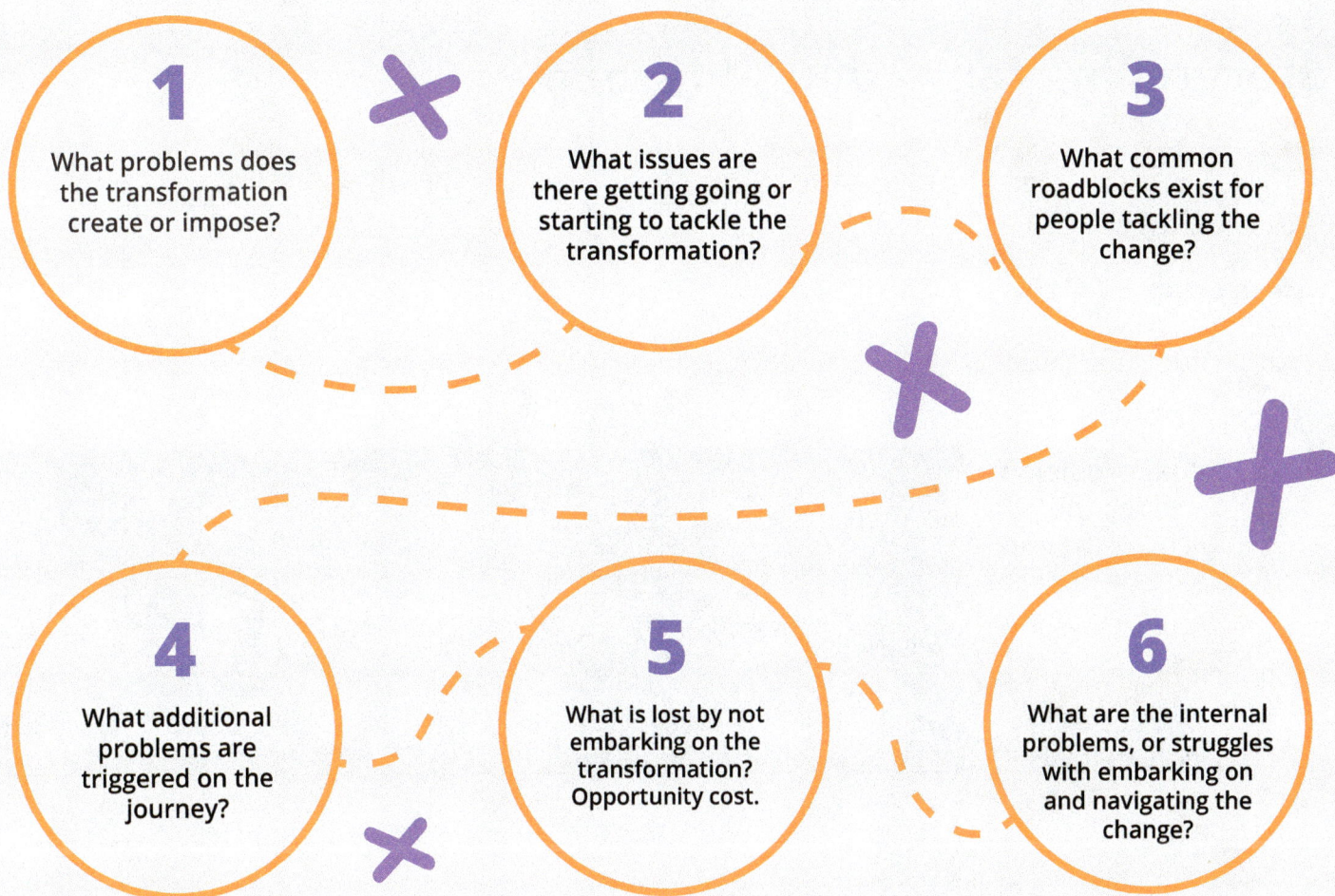

In Queens Gambit, episode 6, our main character, the hero or protagonist, Beth, is an alcoholic. She's made it to the final of a competition, and she lets her guard down. A friend resurfaces in her Parisian hotel and suggests they have a drink. As the audience, we are screaming, "No! Don't do it! You have the final the next day!" What does she do? She has a drink. She makes it to the game late but hungover. She loses the game.

Storytelling for Action™ Playbooks
PROBLEMS – HACKS

What problems does the transformation create or impose?

- Reduction in availability of resources, product, talent.
- Commodity or service price increases.
- Ability to operate in certain markets is restricted or ended.
- How quickly will people or companies fall behind those who embrace the change.
- Does the transformation eliminate any legacy services you rely on? Will it? What's the risk roadmap?

What issues are there getting going or starting to tackle the transformation?

- Perceived high costs.
- Lack of urgency.
- Lack of ability or skillset to act on or manage the change.
- Is it a complex or challenging topic to understand?
- Lack of organizational consensus on the opportunity and risk.

What common roadblocks exist for people tackling the change?

- Pitfalls awaiting the unprepared.
- The failure of others that tried and failed that can be cited.
- Dead ends or risky routes that can delay success.
- Blind spots or lack of preparedness that undermine success.
- Government regulation or policy that impacts the change.
- Misperceptions of time, treasure or technology required.

What additional problems are triggered on the journey?

- New products or technology that breaks old tools or processes.
- The need to obtain approvals, certifications, or licenses.
- Overlap of secondary capabilities with existing investments call into question those investments and force further change.
- Increased competition or press awareness that must be managed.
- Employee and staffing impacts, layoffs, or training costs.

What is lost by not embarking on the transformation? Opportunity cost.

- People or businesses left behind by not embracing the change.
- Evidence of existing business models being put under threat.
- Loss of customers, revenue, or market share.
- Can no longer compete (not responsive, fast enough, high costs).

What are the internal problems, or struggles with embarking on and navigating the change?

- Reskilling Need to reskill to participate.
- No longer certain of the value you bring to your role.
- Negative psychological impact through fear of obsolescence.
- Loss of purpose, meaning or confidence.

Storytelling for Action™ Playbooks

PROBLEMS – WORKSHE

What problems does the transformation create or impose?

What issues are there getting going or starting to tackle the transformation?

What common roadblocks exist for people tackling the change?

What additional problems are triggered on the journey?

What is lost by not embarking on the transformation? Opportunity cost.

What are the internal problems, or struggles with embarking on and navigating the change?

STORIES - OVERVIEW

"If you talk to a man in a language he understands, that goes to his head. If you talk to him in his language, that goes to his heart." – Nelson Mandela

Think of the last time you bought something. Did you browse product reviews late into the night? Social proof helps people avoid mistakes. It also helps them get excited about what their life will be like when they take the plunge.

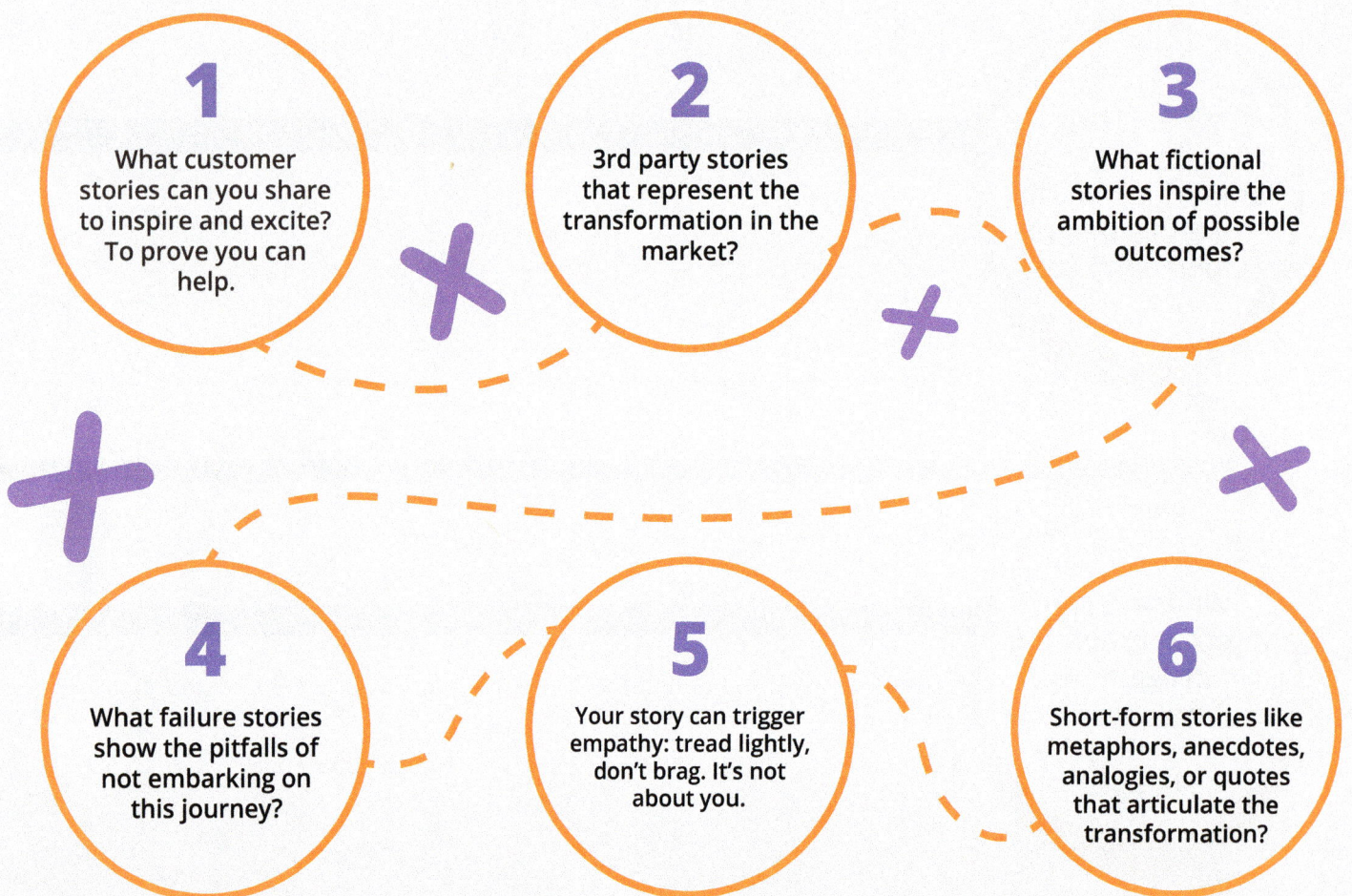

1
What customer stories can you share to inspire and excite? To prove you can help.

2
3rd party stories that represent the transformation in the market?

3
What fictional stories inspire the ambition of possible outcomes?

4
What failure stories show the pitfalls of not embarking on this journey?

5
Your story can trigger empathy: tread lightly, don't brag. It's not about you.

6
Short-form stories like metaphors, anecdotes, analogies, or quotes that articulate the transformation?

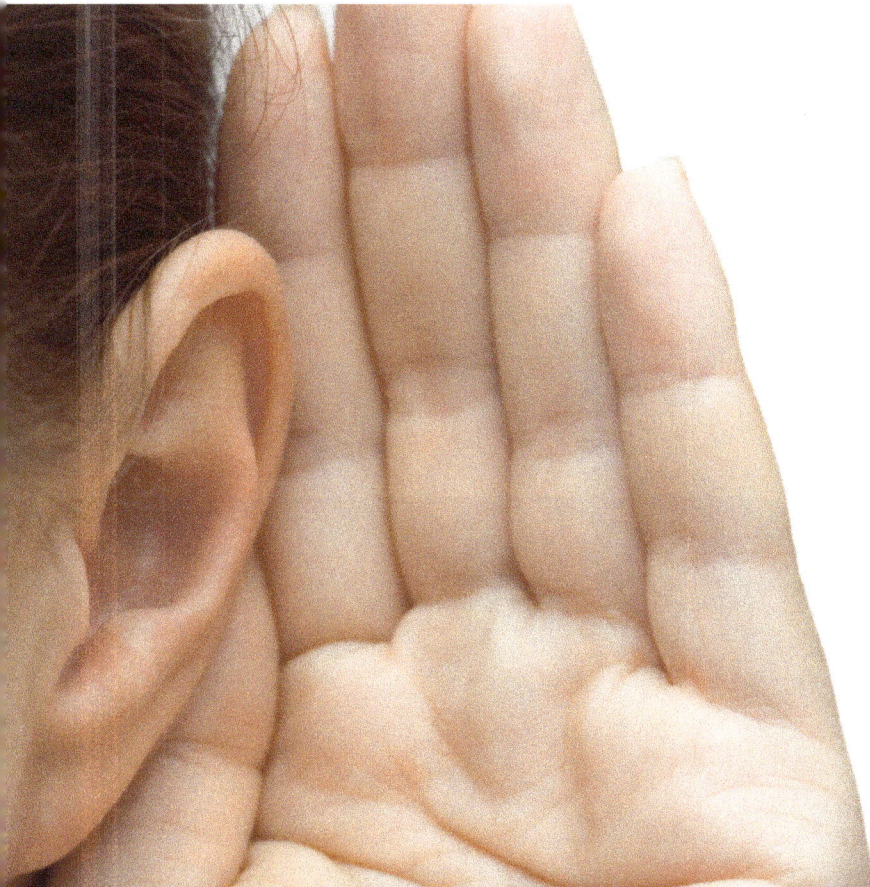

What customer stories can you share to inspire and excite? To prove you can help.

Remember, all stories have people, obstacles to overcome, and outcomes that find the hero in an exciting new or better world. Who are the people that you can help the most?

The Go Narrative 3D Story™ framework can help you break down and tell your stories.

And remember, you are never the hero. The hero is your customer. You are the guide and provider of the secret sauce that helps the ordinary person become the hero.

Storytelling for Action™ Playbooks
STORIES – HACKS

What customer stories can you share to inspire and excite? To show how you help.

- Case studies! Or rather "case stories."
- Lead with their business and their transformation.
- Remember, you are a part of the "denouement," not the hero.
- Social proof quotes.
- Facts from customer surveys.

3rd party stories that represent the transformation in the market?

- Companies or people that successfully tackled the transformation.
- Celebrities that are proponents of tackling the transformation (e.g., Arianna Huffington, Elon Musk, Lisa Su)
- Stories of success from the Early Majority.
- Similar historical transformations that provide a compelling metaphor, e.g., Internet & Telegraph both were communications revolutions.

What fictional stories inspire the ambition of possible outcomes?

- Semi-fiction: remove the names of the innocent (or guilty).
- Hybrid stories of multiple customers crafted as a single story.
- Breathe life into your target personas with "reference stories," like a "reference design," demonstrating realistic situations and believable outcomes.

HACK

What failure stories show the pitfalls of not embarking on this journey?

- Stories that show worst-case scenarios and how to avoid them.
- Demonstrate the opportunity cost of not embracing the change.
- What suffering is introduced to those companies or people who do not embrace the change?
- Timeliness. Will it become more difficult or expensive later?

Your story can trigger empathy: tread lightly, don't brag. It's not about you.

- How and why you invented or designed the product or service.
- Did your company get time or cost savings from the implementation?
- Share your strategic narrative, vision, or mission and the positive change you seek to bring to the world.
- What setbacks or injustice did you overcome to bring the innovation?
- Prioritize people. Don't brag. Don't focus on the product.

Short-form stories like metaphors, anecdotes, analogies, or quotes that articulate the transformation?

- Channel the essence of the narrative as a metaphor. "It's like…"
- …or a simile, or an anecdote.
- Fables can be a proxy for the theme of your narrative.
- Metaphor: Crystal Ball = Prediction, forecasting
- Metaphor: Birds eye view = Seeing the whole problem or picture
- Metaphor: Easy as pie = Ease of use, adoption

Storytelling for Action™ Playbooks
STORIES – WORKSHEET

What customer stories can you share to inspire and excite? To show how you help.

3rd party stories that represent the transformation in the market?

What fictional stories inspire the ambition of possible outcomes?

- WOR

What failure stories show the pitfalls of not embarking on this journey?

Your story can trigger empathy: tread lightly, don't brag. It's not about you.

Short-form stories like metaphors, anecdotes, analogies, or quotes that articulate the transformation?

TRIPS STORYTELLING™

HOW-TO. PUTTING IT ALL TOGETHER. HOW WE APPROACH IT.

A STRATEGIC NARRATIVE ISN'T INVENTED, IT'S _UNCOVERED_

- NARRATIVE AUDIT
- WORKSHOPPING
- CUSTOMER INTERVIEWS
- EXECUTIVE INTERVIEWS

TRIPS & 3D MODELS

- JOB TO BE DONE
- WHY
- PURPOSE
- VALUES
- MISSION
- INSPIRATIONS
- DESIRES
- VISIONS

STRATEGIC NARRATIVE

REFINED
FORGED
SHARPENED

IT'S

CREATE ALIGNMENT

INCREASE DEMAND

ACCELERATE PIPELINE

TAKE

CONTROL

- METAPHORS
- MANIFESTO
- THE WHOLE STORY (LONG STORY NARRATIVE)
- CULTURAL OR HISTORICAL NARRATIVES TO ACCELERATE UNDERSTANDING

STORIES TO QUICKLY HACK MEANING

THE GOLDEN THREAD

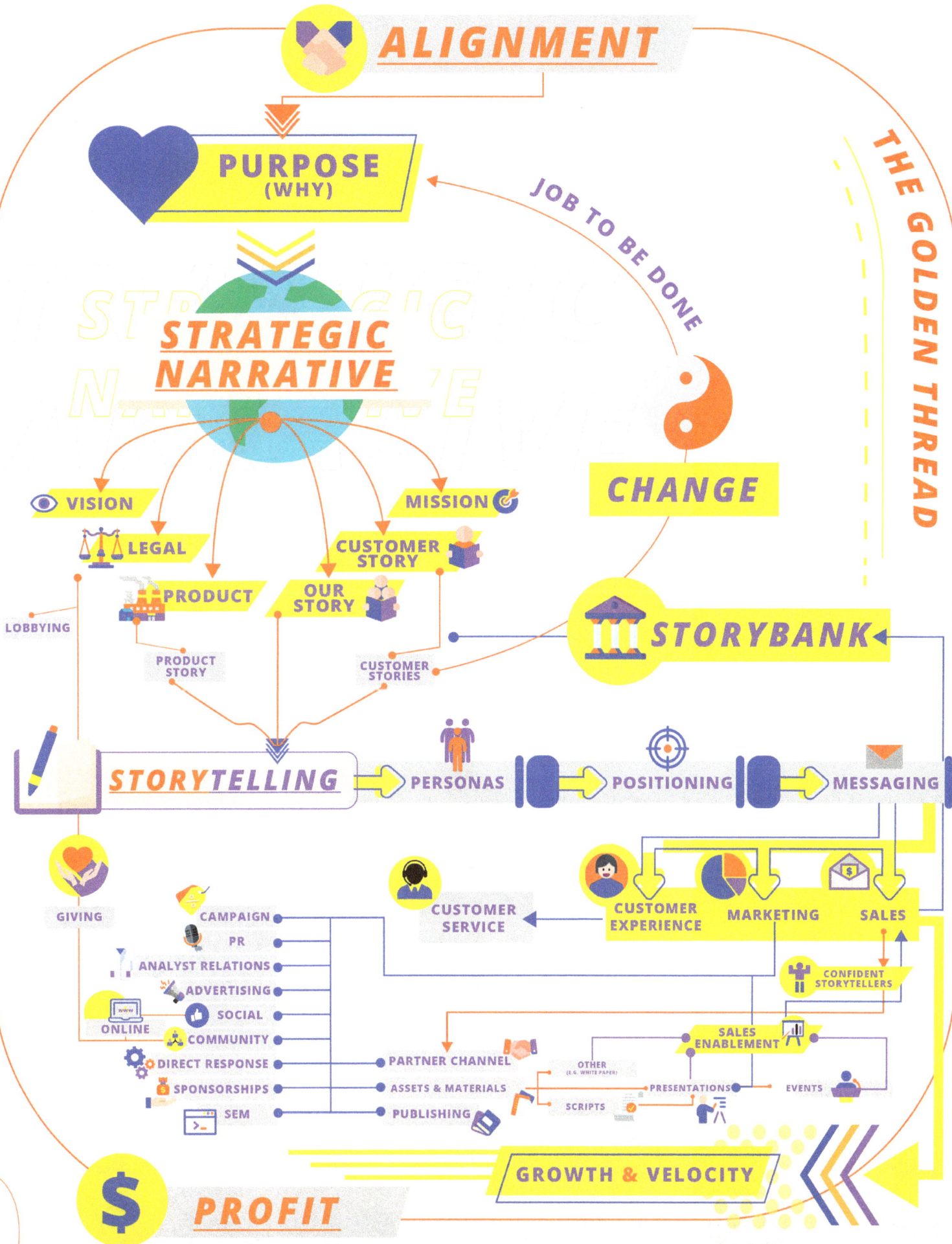

TRIPS STORYTELLING™
STORY TOUCHES THE WHOLE BUSINESS.

ALIGNMENT

PURPOSE (WHY)

STRATEGIC NARRATIVE

JOB TO BE DONE

CHANGE

VISION

MISSION

LEGAL

CUSTOMER STORY

LOBBYING

PRODUCT

OUR STORY

STORYBANK

PRODUCT STORY

CUSTOMER STORIES

THE GOLDEN THREAD

STORYTELLING → PERSONAS → POSITIONING → MESSAGING

GIVING

CAMPAIGN
PR
ANALYST RELATIONS
ADVERTISING
SOCIAL
ONLINE
COMMUNITY
DIRECT RESPONSE
SPONSORSHIPS
SEM

CUSTOMER SERVICE

CUSTOMER EXPERIENCE

MARKETING

SALES

CONFIDENT STORYTELLERS

PARTNER CHANNEL

ASSETS & MATERIALS

PUBLISHING

OTHER (E.G. WHITE PAPER)

SCRIPTS

PRESENTATIONS

SALES ENABLEMENT

EVENTS

GROWTH & VELOCITY

$ PROFIT

THE NARRATIVE FORG
YOUR STORY TO LIFE

"There's nothing you can do that can't be done.
Nothing you can sing that can't be sung.
Nothing you can say, but you can learn how to play the game."– The Beatles

What's next? You may be thinking. You've collected the head, the heart, and the soul of your brand, product, or campaign.

Now it's time to put that raw material to use.

FORGING IS AN ART AND A SCIENCE.

You want your narrative to be accurate, interesting, and engaging.

Your mission is to facilitate understanding and alignment in all you do. And to which all your customers are exposed.

BRINGING

When there is alignment in all you say and do, there is integrity. When there is integrity, there is authenticity and the opportunity to deliver amazing customer experiences.

THE NARRATIVE FORGE – HOW TO CRAFT A STRATEGIC NARRATIVE

Third-party validation is essential. Performing original research will help you validate your hypothesis. In addition to your team's input, **make sure you speak to customers**. You can use this to prototype research that you run as surveys and focus groups to a broader audience.

We also suggest performing an Environmental Trend Scan. This process looks at your category and how people research and buy within it. For what are they looking? How are they searching? How are other brands acting and speaking in the market?

Weave these inputs into something that resonates and engages your audience. **What shortcuts to understanding exist?** Think of your favorite song and the meaning it implies through metaphor and analogy. Look to the zeitgeist and history. What is happening or has happened which is a metaphor for your narrative? What stories represent that narrative? Just like a songwriter, you are leveraging things people understand already to help them understand your brand.

While you may eventually create a video or presentation to help communicate your strategic narrative, writing it first is essential. Writing clarifies your narrative to connect all the most essential ideas.

When you write, you simplify, and pressure test your ideas. The written word is stark and clear and ready for you to gain stakeholder's agreement. And finally, it becomes an authentic record of focus for everything your company says and does—the golden thread.

RATIVE F

A STRA

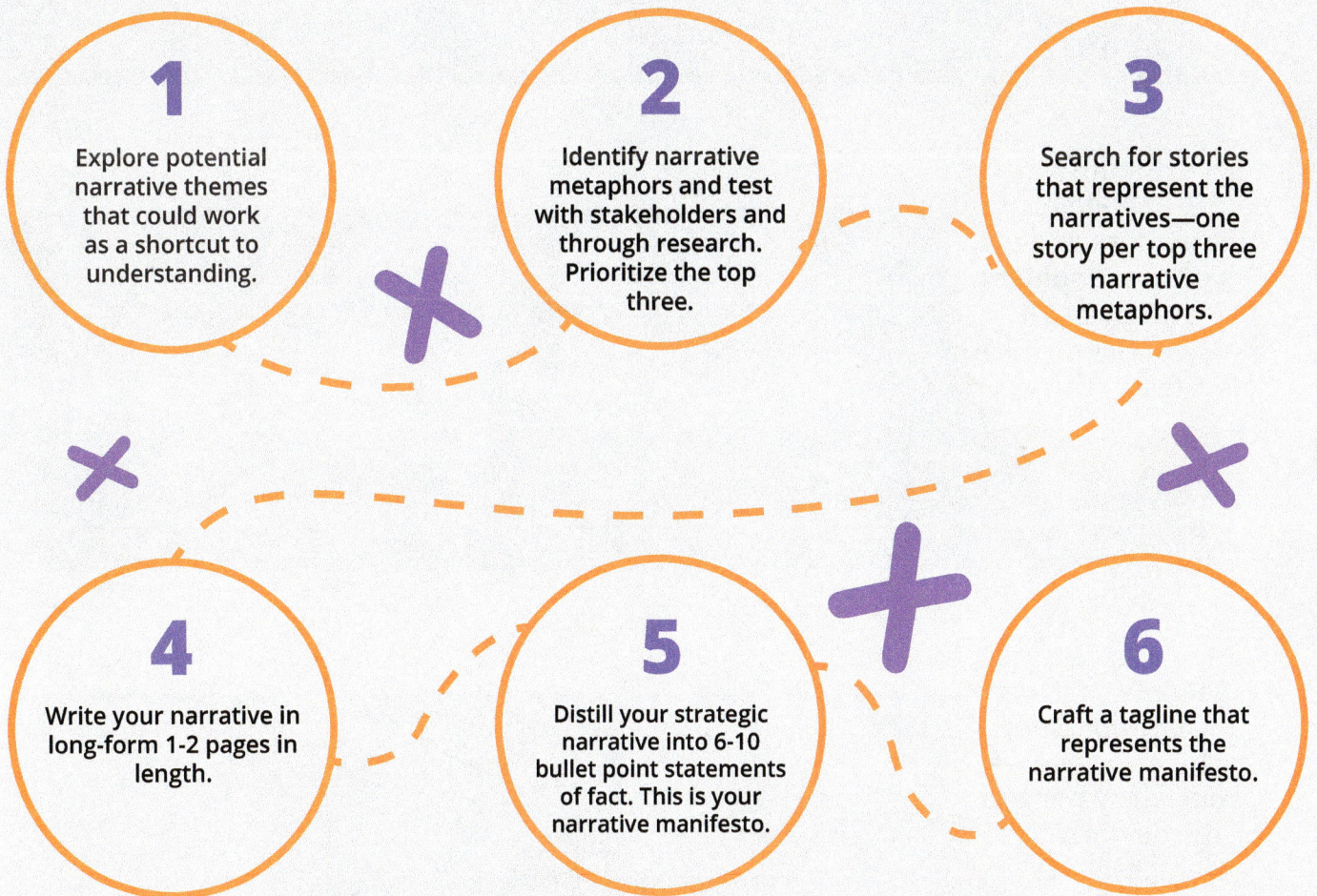

1

Explore potential narrative themes that could work as a shortcut to understanding.

2

Identify narrative metaphors and test with stakeholders and through research. Prioritize the top three.

3

Search for stories that represent the narratives—one story per top three narrative metaphors.

4

Write your narrative in long-form 1-2 pages in length.

5

Distill your strategic narrative into 6-10 bullet point statements of fact. This is your narrative manifesto.

6

Craft a tagline that represents the narrative manifesto.

Storytelling for Action™ Playbooks
STRATEGIC NARRATIVE

Explore potential narrative themes that could work as a shortcut to understanding.

- Consider the general point or purpose. Here are some examples:
  - Improvement related: faster, better, stronger.
  - Quality related: the best, the most reliable, customer service.
  - Purpose: make the world better, help a particular group.
  - People: community engagement, individual success.
  - Where on Maslow's hierarchy do you serve? Saftey? Purpose?

Identify narrative metaphors and test with stakeholders and through research. Prioritize the top three.

- "It's like..."
- Zeitgeist: is something happening in the world you align to?
- History: are you doing something like a prior human achievement?
- Consider people, cultures, countries, organizations, inventions.
- Look both within and outside of your industry.

Search for stories that represent the narratives— one story per top three narrative metaphors.

- Major events: wars, pandemics, discoveries, inventions.
- Whose story is it?
- What did they want?
- What stood in the way?
- How did they change or succeed?

HACKS

Write your narrative in long-form 1-2 pages in length.

- Use the 3D Story™ framework for structure.
- Tell it through the eyes of a real or imagined customer.
- Show the why and any struggle involved by those in your company in bringing the world what your company delivers.
- Use stories from the prior step to make your point.
- Weave in the metaphor e.g., if the narrative metaphor was "Quality Control" find ways to include quality throughout your narrative.

Distill your strategic narrative into 6-10 bullet point statements of fact. This is your narrative manifesto.

- Identify 6-10 key points to distill through the narrative.
- Create active imperative statements that represent your narrative.
- "Because of...." | "We believe in...." | "It is known that..." | "Only through _____ can we...." | "With _____ we must...."
- Flow: each statement should build on or result from the prior.
- End on a final statement that directly uses your narrative metaphor

Craft a tagline that represents the narrative manifesto.

- Look back to your narrative theme and the narrative metaphor
- Review the narrative manifesto
- Craft a single statement that is representative of the manifesto using the theme of the metaphor

GoNarrative
Get Attention. Be Heard. Sell More.

2022 EDITION
RECIPE AND
INGREDIENTS INCLUDED
• 14 HOW-TO FLOW
• OVER 300 HACK

PRESENTATION HACKS
STORYTELLING FOR ACTION™ PLAYBOOK

BUILD PRESENTATIONS THAT **MOVE PEOPLE** TO ACT EVEN WITH LIMITED TIME.

FROM PITCH DECKS TO WEBINARS. **ALL BENEFIT FROM STORY**.

WARNING:
Not for Screenwriters or Novelists

Storytelling for Action™ Playbooks

PLAYBOOK COLLECTION

Our Storytelling For Action™ playbooks are designed as practical guides to help you benefit from the power of storytelling without becoming a storytelling expert.

Each playbook stands alone. They also work together as an all-up master playbook.

1
3D STORY™ MODEL
Tell consistent, impactful stories with this one-stop shop to telling business stories.

2
STORY MEET™ METHOD
Craft stories that engage people and retain their attention with the suitable types of emotions.

3
TRIPS STORYTELLING™ FRAMEWORK
Create aligned stories that connect to the business and drive impact.

4
STORYTELLING HACKS: PRESENTATIONS (THIS PLAYBOOK)
Build presentations that move people to act even with limited time.

5
STORYTELLING HACKS: CASE STUDIES
Demonstrate social proof with customer stories without getting hung up on product details.

6
STORYTELLING HACKS: SHORT-FORM CONTENT
Make even the shortest content pop despite limited space.

STORYTELLING FOR PRESENTATIONS

"Death. By. PowerPoint" is a trope for a reason.

The "Death By" narrative is that presentations are deathly dull.

We've all got a story where we experienced nodding off in the throng of an audience as the presenter fails to capture and maintain our attention.

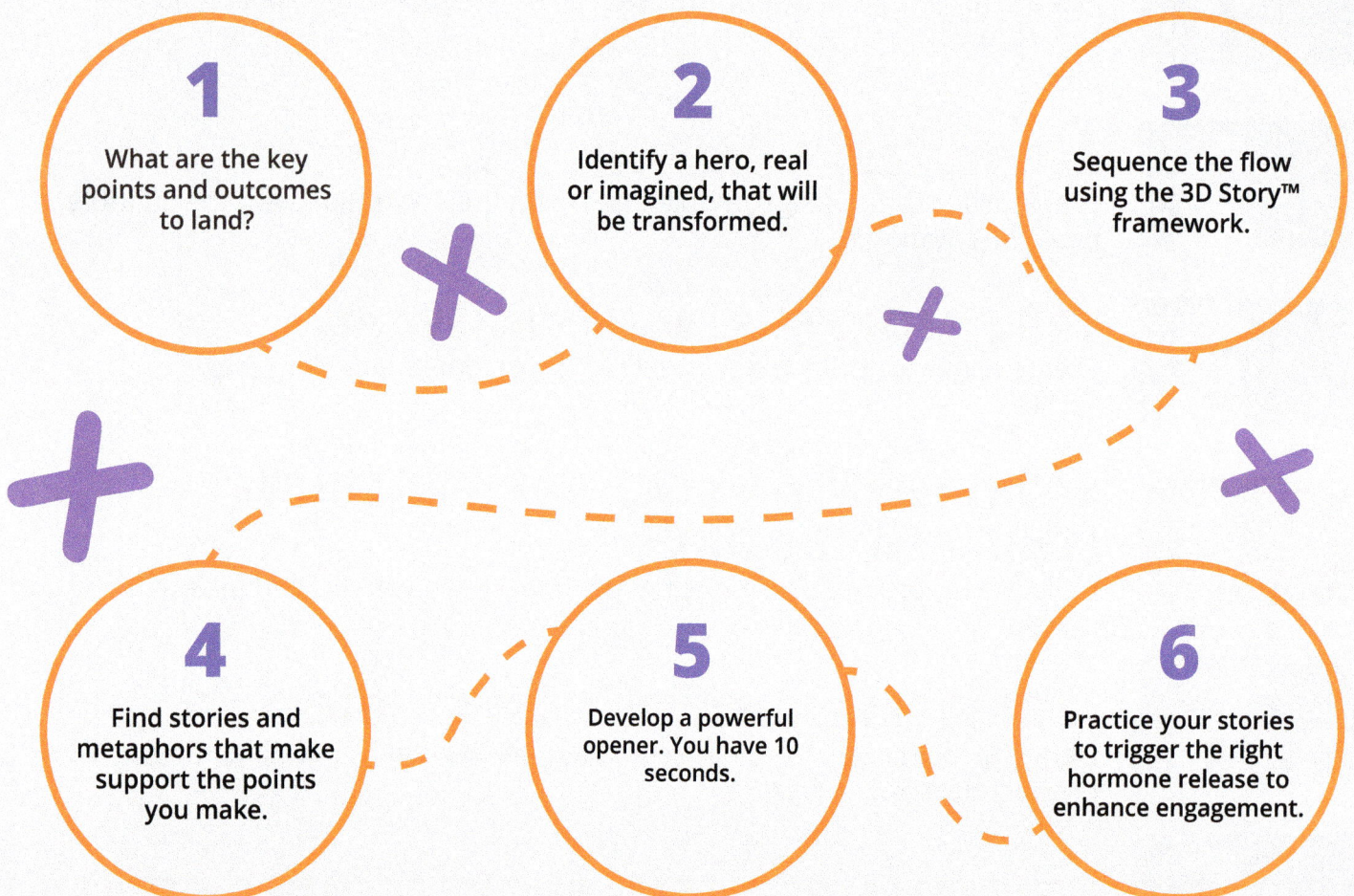

1 What are the key points and outcomes to land?

2 Identify a hero, real or imagined, that will be transformed.

3 Sequence the flow using the 3D Story™ framework.

4 Find stories and metaphors that make support the points you make.

5 Develop a powerful opener. You have 10 seconds.

6 Practice your stories to trigger the right hormone release to enhance engagement.

CTION™
ENTATIONS

Presentations need to start with a bang. They need great delivery. They need stories throughout. They need a strong story flow. They need to have a narrative.

Being respectful of the audience's time requires three essentials (1) Capture and retain their attention, (2) Be interesting and relevant, (3) Get them to take action, a next step after the presentation.

Bonus tip: write your script first then put your slides to the script.

Storytelling for Action™ Playbooks
PRESENTATION - HACK

What are the key points and outcomes to land?

- Begin with the end in mind: what will someone gain by acting on your presentation?
- Develop a clear objective: e.g., excite, educate, sell.
- What should they remember? Better life? A fact? A "how-to.'
- Draw from your Denouement and Transformation work.

Identify a hero, real or imagined, that will be transformed.

- What are their traits?
- What are they running from? Towards?
- What do they want? Better, faster, stronger?
- Draw from your Desire, Difficulty and Problems work.
- What stands in their way? Is there a villain?
- Place your hero in the world and the transformation being imposed.

Sequence the flow using the 3D Story™ framework.

- Create contrast moments throughout (before/after, good/bad).
- Intro: state the desire, the difficulty, and the denouement.
- Body: contrast difficulty and denouement, the opportunity cost not acting. Resist sharing your product until the halfway point.
- Close: restate the desire, difficulty, and denouement. Clearly show the action steps to execute the transformation.

TATION

Find stories and metaphors that make support the points you make.

- Identify a story or metaphor for each objective or memorable item.
- Leverage Stories from your TRIPS Storytelling™ legwork.
- For each story, create a mini 3D™ Story for each point to be made "People want ___ But ___ stands in the way. This is resolved through ___ and ___ (your product) resulting in _____."

Develop a powerful opener. You have 10 seconds.

- You have 10 seconds to capture their attention.
- Select the most powerful story from the stories you have selected.
- Select an authentic story from your life that shows how you were exposed to the transformation you are taking them on. "The first time you..." learned this, discovered, saw the impact that is possible. It's like a children's story's "Once upon a time..."

Practice your stories to trigger the right hormone release to enhance engagement.

- Pauses, cliffhangers, and twists release dopamine which help with focus, memory, and motivation.
- Struggle triggers cortisol resulting in attention. Use sparingly.
- Authentic stories trigger oxytocin, bonding you with your audience.
- Setback stories trigger serotonin fostering empathy and memory.
- Funny stories and anecdotes trigger endorphins and good feelings.

Storytelling for Action™ Playbooks
PRESENTATION - WOR|

What are the key points and outcomes to land?

Identify a hero, real or imagined, that will be transformed.

Sequence the flow using the 3D Story™ framework.

TATION

SHEET

Find stories and metaphors that make support the points you make.

Develop a powerful opener. You have 10 seconds.

Practice your stories to trigger the right hormone release to enhance engagement.

2022 EDITIO
RECIPE AN
INGREDIENTS INCLUDE
• 14 HOW-TO FLOW
• OVER 300 HACK

CASE ~~STUDIES~~
STORY HACKS
STORYTELLING FOR ACTION™
PLAYBOOK

DEMONSTRATE **SOCIAL PROOF** WITH CUSTOMER STORIES **WITHOUT GETTING HUNG UP** ON PRODUCT DETAILS.

OUR OLD **"SOCIAL PROOF"** FRIEND **MADE BETTER** WITH STORIES.

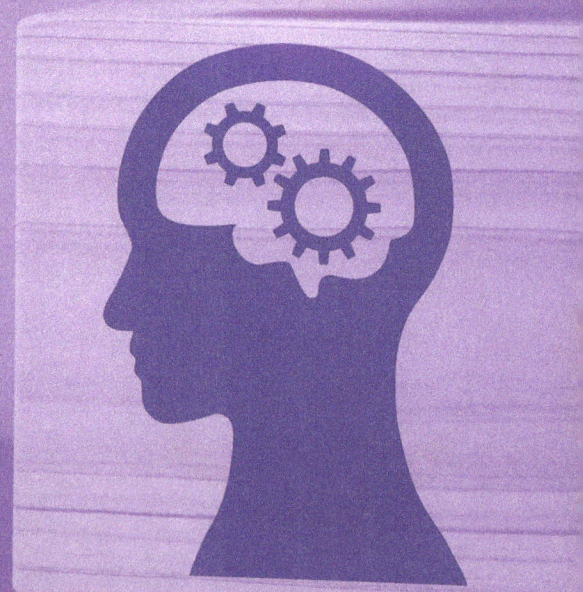

WARNING: Not for Screenwriters or Novelists

Storytelling for Action™ Playbooks

PLAYBOOK COLLECTION

Our Storytelling For Action™ playbooks are designed as practical guides to help you benefit from the power of storytelling without becoming a storytelling expert.

Each playbook stands alone. They also work together as an all-up master playbook.

1 3D STORY™ MODEL
Tell consistent, impactful stories with this one-stop shop to telling business stories.

2 STORY MEET™ METHOD
Craft stories that engage people and retain their attention with the suitable types of emotions.

3 TRIPS STORYTELLING™ FRAMEWORK
Create aligned stories that connect to the business and drive impact.

4 STORYTELLING HACKS: PRESENTATIONS
Build presentations that move people to act even with limited time.

5 STORYTELLING HACKS: CASE STUDIES (THIS PLAYBOOK)
Demonstrate social proof with customer stories without getting hung up on product details.

6 STORYTELLING HACKS: SHORT-FORM CONTENT
Make even the shortest content pop despite limited space.

STORYTELLING FOR A
CASE STUDIES - OVER

Five stars! Product Reviews. Restaurant reviews. Review culture is the new norm. But social proof has always been the way.

This is particularly strong in the early majority market who reference other members in that segment. They don't want to be the first to buy. And they want to know what they are getting into.

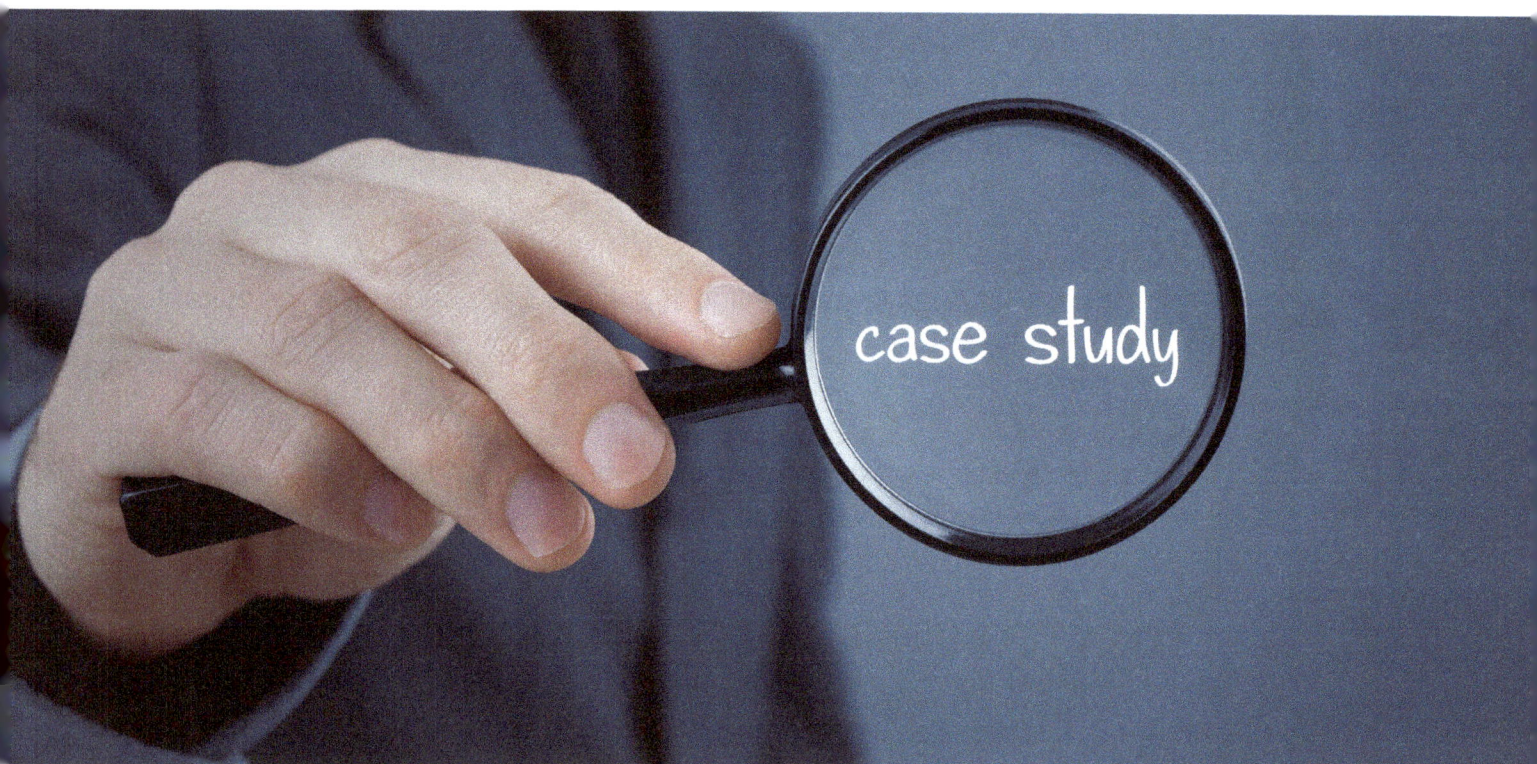

Case studies are often horrific, hard-to-read, self-serving long-form content.

Case studies usually scream out for which brand they were created. The company logo is on the asset, and it is usually downloaded from the brand's website. Don't waste valuable real estate talking about you. Your prospective customers want to hear about people like them who have found success.

TION™
EW

1
Work with sales and customer success to identify target customers.

2
Select the right customers.

3
Take an outside-in, journalistic approach.

4
Structure with 3D Story™ framework.

5
Put your company and product in its place.

6
Slice and dice the big "turkey" content into multiple dishes for use across the customer journey.

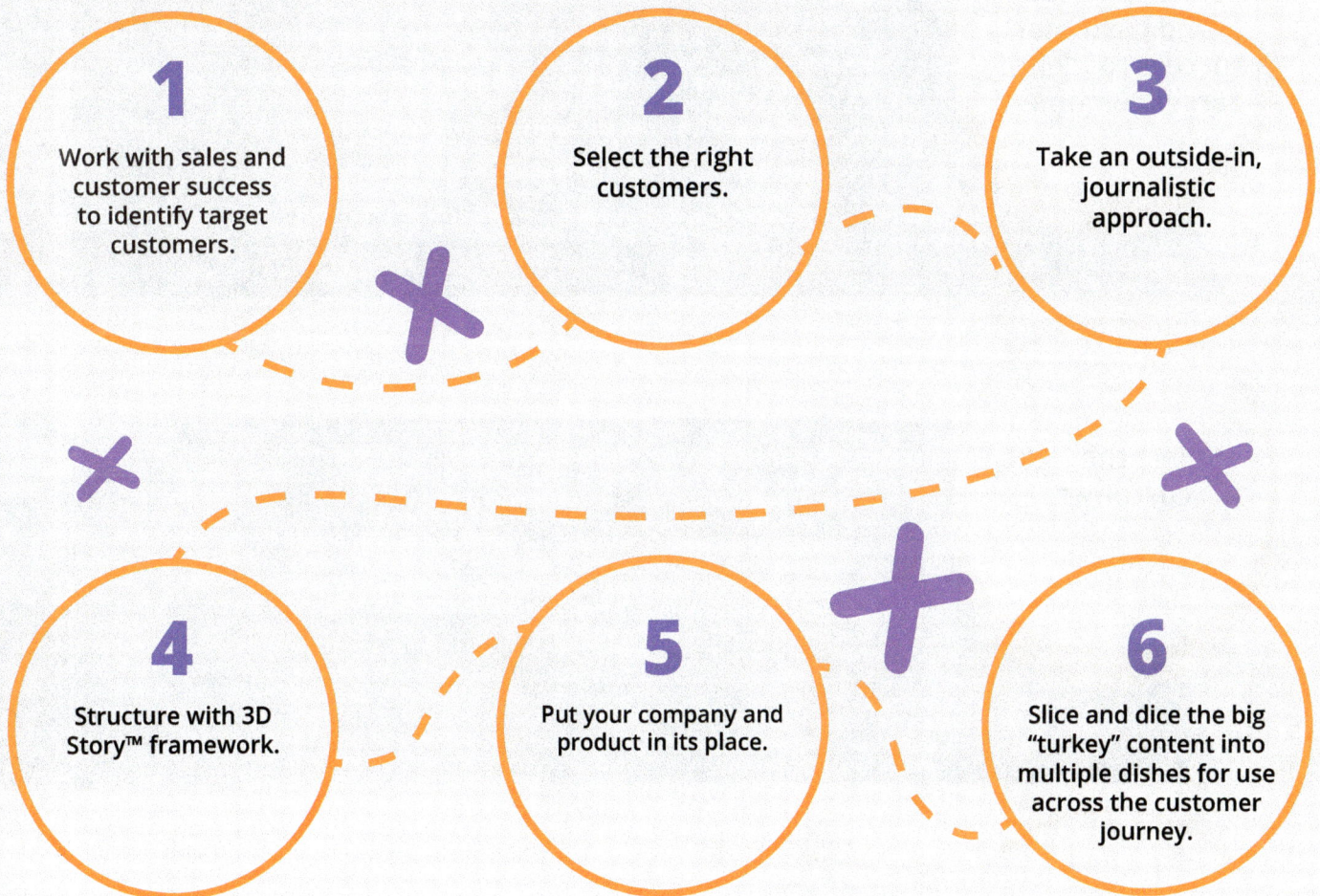

Nowadays, you can make the most of technology to diversify your case study content through videos, infographics, and more. It's also true that long-form can support the purchase journey if it's well constructed and written.

Storytelling for Action™ Playbooks

CASE STUDY - HACKS

Work with sales and customer success to identify target customers.

- Partner with sales and customer success teams.
- Develop low friction, rewarding processes for sales to submit stories.
- Consider gives & gets – you will give the customer content so good they will want to share it, you will promote their brand on your site.
- Ideally select customers where a firm outcome or metric can be cited.
- Respect their concerns: companies may not allow for exact numbers or results to be used due to legal or competitive reasons.

Select the right customers.

- Which customers did you help navigate the Transformation in a way that produced meaningful results?
- Big brands help validate your social proof.
- People love underdog stories; look for those too.
- Select customers who can commit to a clear, timely approval process.

Take an outside-in, journalistic approach.

- Repeat after me: it's about them, not us. Make this your mantra.
- Seek out, capture, and articulate the company's purpose.
- Deploy a journalistic approach; look for the compelling stories a click or two below the surface.
- Feature real people wherever possible. Frame them as becoming a hero for their company through the story you tell.

UDY - H

Structure with 3D Story™ framework

- Approach the case study as telling their story
- Desire: what do/did they want, what's their mission?
- Difficulty: what is/was standing in their way achieving this?
- Denouement: how did they untangle the knot (you are mentioned here). Consider the big picture: approach they used, internal processes, challenges, roadblocks, and 3rd party services or products.

Put your company and product in its place.

- A box of cereal doesn't list the ingredients on the front. Don't lead with your company or product.
- Weave in your company, product, or service at the right time; during the denouement as a part of their solution.
- How did you make them proud of choosing you?
- Draw out emotionally engaging soft statements; what did it feel like to work with your company?

Slice and dice the big "turkey" content into multiple dishes for use across the customer journey.

- Early journey: ads, sponsorships, landing pages
- Late journey: "how-to" implementation guide, infographics
- Social: feature individuals, pepper across the editorial calendar
- Quotes: websites, presentations
- Events: keynote (excite) and breakout session guests (explain)

Storytelling for Action™ Playbooks

CASE STUDY – WORKSH

Work with sales and customer success to identify target customers.

Select the right customers.

Take an outside-in, journalistic approach.

ET UDY - W

Structure with 3D Story™ framework

Put your company and product in its place.

Slice and dice the big "turkey" content into multiple dishes for use across the customer journey.

GoNarrative

2022 EDITION
RECIPE AN
INGREDIENTS INCLUDED
• 14 HOW-TO FLOW
• OVER 300 HACK

SHORT-FORM HACKS
STORYTELLING FOR ACTION™
PLAYBOOK

MAKE EVEN THE SHORTEST CONTENT POP *DESPITE LIMITED SPACE.*

GET **FROM LONG-FORM TO DISTILLED** *BITE-SIZED STORY GOODNESS IN MINUTES.*

WARNING:
Not for Screenwriters
or Novelists

Storytelling for Action™ Playbooks

PLAYBOOK COLLECTION

Our Storytelling For Action™ playbooks are designed as practical guides to help you benefit from the power of storytelling without becoming a storytelling expert.

Each playbook stands alone. They also work together as an all-up master playbook.

1 3D STORY™ MODEL
Tell consistent, impactful stories with this one-stop shop to telling business stories.

2 STORY MEET™ METHOD
Craft stories that engage people and retain their attention with the suitable types of emotions.

3 TRIPS STORYTELLING™ FRAMEWORK
Create aligned stories that connect to the business and drive impact.

4 STORYTELLING HACKS: PRESENTATIONS
Build presentations that move people to act even with limited time.

5 STORYTELLING HACKS: CASE STUDIES
Demonstrate social proof with customer stories without getting hung up on product details.

6 STORYTELLING HACKS: SHORT-FORM CONTENT (THIS PLAYBOOK)
Make even the shortest content pop despite limited space.

STORYTELLING FOR A
SHORT-FORM - OVERV

The shorter it is, the harder it is to craft and the more potent it is. Distillation is a craft that must be connected to the big picture to be effective.

"Just do it." "Desire. Difficulty. Denouement." Because our brains work by association, they rapidly go to work trying to make sense of things.

This results in us inferring meaning. It's why we use one metaphor for every eleven seconds of speech. It's also why we need that 'big picture' house in order to get the small stuff right.

Brevity is brutal, picking the right words to trigger the right kind of meaning (the recipient ultimately owns interpretation).

When you hear Nike's famous "Just do it" slogan, you put yourself in a story; of making an effort, to get something done with no excuses.

1

Identify an audience.

2

Determine the campaign goals.

3

Select a campaign-specific narrative theme.

4

Craft a 3D Story™ tale of real personas that the campaign targets.

5

Sequencing: Identify the actions in which you want your short-form item to result.

6

Craft content to encourage prospects to take each action.

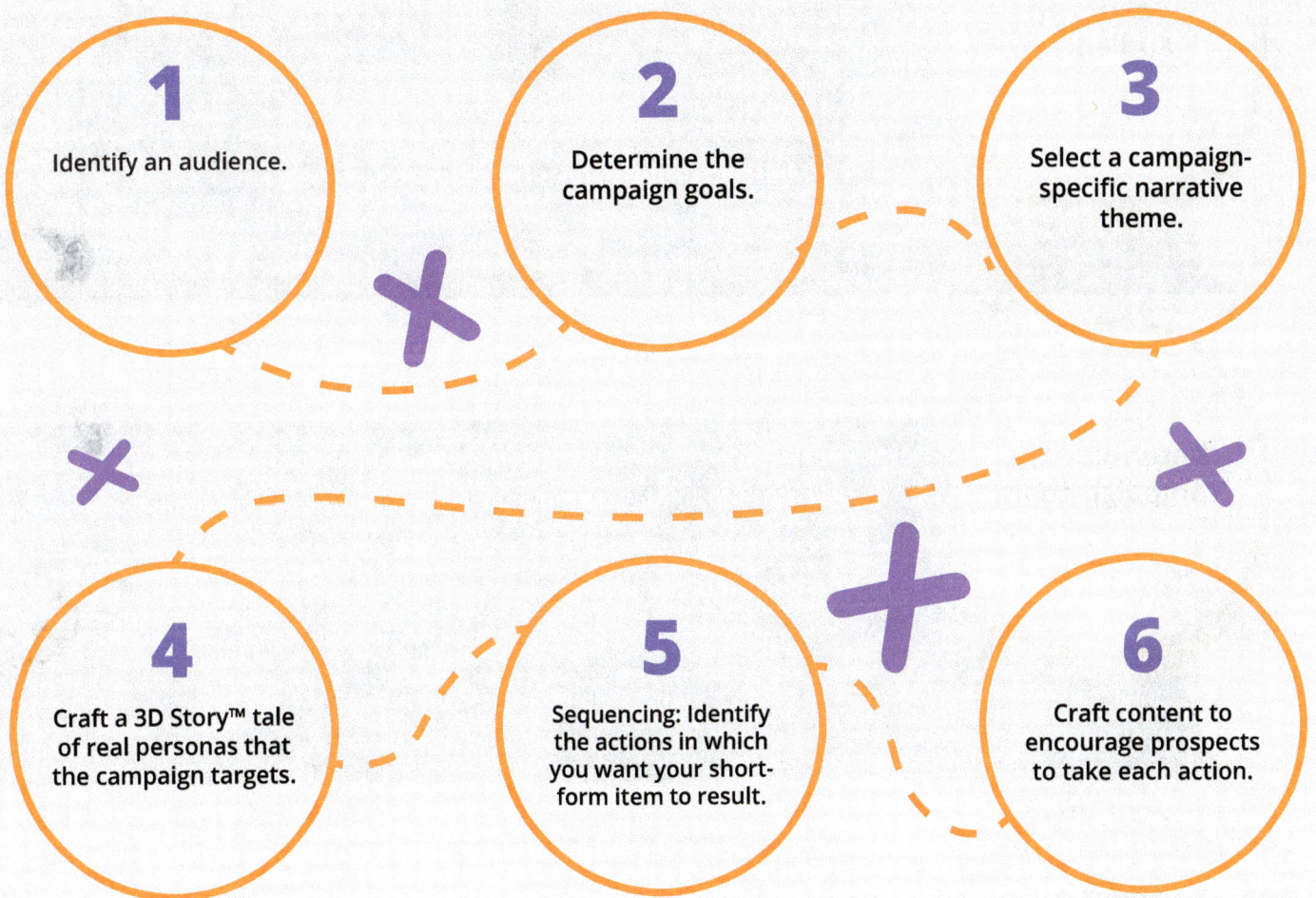

Because you defined your TRIPS Storytelling™ narrative framework, you should already have the raw material you need. And if you and your team crafted your strategic narrative, you will have the guard rails to prepare meaningful triggers.

Storytelling for Action™ Playbooks
SHORT FORM – HACKS

Identify an audience.

- In this thought experiment we'll be focused on Business Intelligence software.
- Targeting CFOs roles.
- Roles vary e.g., public, private companies, big, small. Let's pick CFOs in Midsized firms in the international trade market.
- Tip: Well researched personas help bring flavor to the stories because each persona will have differing needs and experiences.

Determine the campaign goals.

- Let's say we're planning a campaign that helps people understand how the software helps with business forecasting.
- Select the improved task e.g., data processing and cleaning.
- Identify how the task is improved e.g., sped up, more accurate.
- Determine any audience wants or needs met by the campaign.

Select a campaign specific narrative theme.

- Let's say our strategic narrative's metaphor for   our fictional Business Intelligence company is "A crystal ball sees all."
- From this let's say we select "Fiscal Clarity" as the campaign specific narrative theme.

ORM -

Craft a 3D Story™ tale of real personas that the campaign targets.

- Desire: Frank, CFO of Weinheftner, wants confidence in his forecasts in a complex trading environment. He relies on many data sources.
- Difficultly: Ineffective data hygiene damages forecast accuracy. Frank fears being caught of guard when presenting to the board, yet again.
- Denouement: Frank confidently guides cost cutting that improves Weinheftner's bottom with speed an accuracy using the latest in AI data processing. All while avoiding that situation again.

Sequencing: Identify the actions in which you want your short-form item to result.

- Headlines. Tweets. Ad copy. They all serve a purpose for a next action in a customers decision journey.
- Identify the action steps required to move along the journey.
- Is the action to subscribe to a newsletter, join a community, see a demo, get a specific outcome (e.g., be more confident), learn how-to do something, make a purchase, satisfy a need (e.g., manage many data sources), download an asset.

Craft content to encourage prospects to take each action.

- You may include all elements in one statement for example a landing page may say "You want confidence in your data and fear being caught off guard. Learn how to automatically connect and cleanse many data sources by downloading our new eBook."
- An advert might be "Confidence in your cleansed data."
- A short, snappy Nikeesque tagline may be "Clean Data Confidence"

Storytelling for Action™ Playbooks
SHORT FORM – WORKS

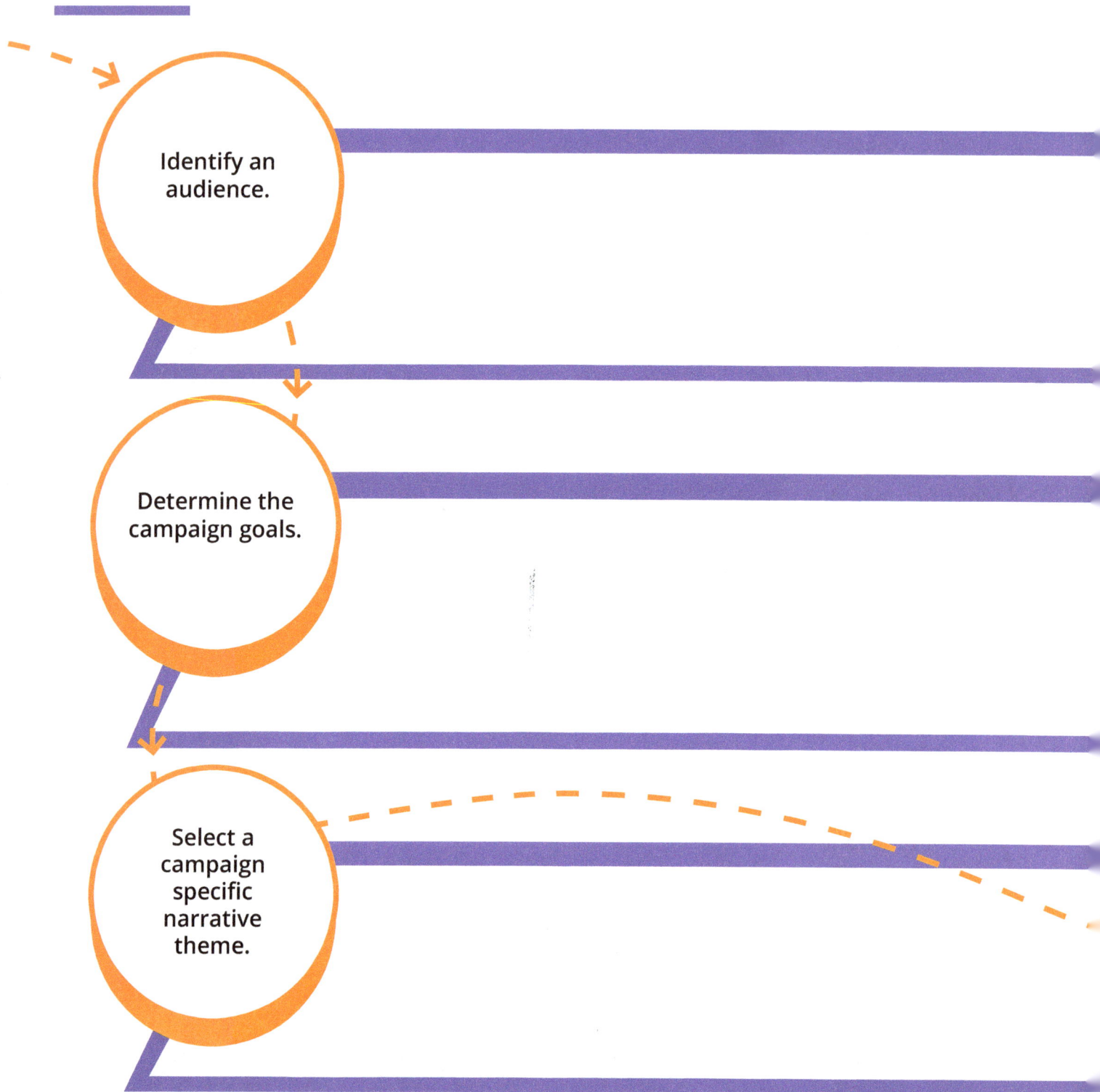

Identify an audience.

Determine the campaign goals.

Select a campaign specific narrative theme.

FORM
EET

Craft a 3D Story™ tale of real personas that the campaign targets.

Sequencing: Identify the actions in which you want your short-form item to result.

Craft content to encourage prospects to take each action.

THANK YOU!

WE HOPE YOU HAVE ENJOYED USING THIS PLAYBOOK TO MAKE THE MOST OF BUSINESS STORYTELLING.

DON'T FORGET TO ENJOY ALL THE PLAYBOOKS

1   3D Story™ model – tell consistent, impactful stories

2   Story MeET™ method – craft stories that engage

3   TRIPS Storytelling™ framework – create alignment

4   Storytelling Hacks: Presentations – presentation stories

5   Storytelling Hacks: Case Studies – case stories

6   Storytelling Hacks: Short-Form Content – short content

If you need further guidance, support or would like us to help you with your business storytelling please reach out to gnhelp@gonarrative.com

Besides, we'd love to hear your story… #StoryAddict

Storytelling for Action™ by Go Narrative